The Swallow: A Novel Based Upon The Actual Experiences Of One Of The Survivors Of The Famous Lafayette Escadrille

Ruth Dunbar

THE SWALLOW

A NOVEL BASED UPON THE
ACTUAL EXPERIENCES OF ONE
OF THE SURVIVORS OF THE
FAMOUS LAFAYETTE ESCADRILLE

BY

RUTH DUNBAR

BONI AND LIVERIGHT
NEW YORK · 1919

(RECAP)

3723
45
.389   (sw

TO MY MOTHER

"THE BRAVEST SOLDIER I HAVE EVER KNOWN"

THE SWALLOW

THE SWALLOW

CHAPTER I

MY mother's father was a captain in the Civil War. Had my mother been a man she, too, would have been a captain—perhaps in a less bloody business. As one of that gentler, fiercer sex, however, she was the wife of a clergyman in a Texas town. But her soul came marching on. Her overcoming spirit—that was my inheritance.

That her spirit in me should seek satisfaction thousands of yards above the German trenches was an accident of time and invention. The Great War and the airplane only gave it direction. The spirit was always there.

My one boyish ambition was to fight. My one boyish regret was that I never could see General Grant. And when airplanes came into use, all my desire crystallised into the one desire to fly. As this presented difficulties to a small boy in a

1

town where flying machines had never been seen, I had to content my martial impulse by attending a military school at home. While I was waiting to become old enough to enter West Point my father died. So I had to withdraw my application and think of some way to help my mother. It was due to her foresight that my decision fell where it did.

"Hard times will affect the sale of breastpins but not of beans," she said. "Think of something people can't do without."

"Bread," I suggested.

"Then start a bakery," she said.

So I went up to the fort where I had always gone to dance with the officers' daughters and had the baker teach me to make bread. During the last few summers I had clerked, driven delivery cars and learned various lower ropes of commerce. As a result I could now handle the business end of my own venture while my mother planned the policy.

"You may as well point your nose at money," was another of her theories. "It costs less to sell ten loaves at ten cents apiece than twenty loaves at five cents apiece."

With this advantage in view we made fashionable bread. We even made bread fashionable.

We sold every loaf for ten cents straight and sold it sealed in the first waxed paper wrappers that had ever come into El Paso. We kept the bakery white as a lily. We had started to supply only a limited demand. But as our custom grew and our machinery kept pace with it we startled our public with noodle-soup and pot-pies and other dishes through which my mother had a enjoyed local fame. And every Saturday evening at six we sold pans of her hot, golden-brown biscuits that became a sacred institution in the homes of El Paso. Soon I had to add my younger brother and my cousin to the staff. We were making a good living for the four of us and turning every surplus cent back into the business.

Then something happened in Europe. A gallant rabbit stood between the hole where its babies trembled, and a band of coyotes. France and England placed themselves beside the rabbit. I waited for America to go in with France and England. America did not do it. But I for one could not go on selling ten-cent loaves in waxed paper. It was my chance, the chance of every young man in America, to adventure generously.

That was August, August of 1914. By Christmas I was still scheming how to get to France. For as I did not want to take money from the business, I should have to work my passage. It was Lee Malone who solved the problem.

My friendship for Lee was founded on one plank: we were after the same girl. Lee had read an advertisement in a New Orleans paper calling for men to work their passage across the sea.

"So if we can get work," said he, coming up to the bakery to show me the paper, "I'll go with you."

I wrung his hand joyfully. To have companionship would double the fun. Besides—this was an afterthought—I should be glad to have him away from El Paso.

I wrote at once to the New Orleans man, whom I shall call Marks. Marks replied that as ships were going out every few days he could use us any time. So it was settled that we were to leave on New Year's night. After a last evening with mother I was to pick Lee up at Jasmine Gray's.

My mother had never tried to keep me. "If I were a young man I'd go, too," she said with that rare heroism that can face hardship for loved ones. Her courage only made the parting more bitter. And when I put my arms about her for a last kiss, it was I, not she, who could not keep back the tears.

"God bless you, wherever you go," she said, pulling my head to her shoulder with a quick pressure before she unclasped my arms to let me go.

I wiped my eyes and, trying to whistle the lump out of my throat, bounded up the steps of the Gray's old Moorish home.

Pausing before the bell I took off my hat and passed a hand over my hair which, always pulling against the wind with the ruffled determination of a hungry carrion, had earned me the title of Buzzard. This, added to the fact that my short-sighted parents, though bearing the name of Byrd, had not scrupled to christen me Richard, produced the tragedy of my childhood. It was bad enough not to have been called General Grant; but the Dicky-bird was not to be borne. In my extreme youth, between the ages of four and eight, I could employ the same method on both sexes for the protection of my honour. In later years public sentiment forced me to cease battering the noses of little girls. But through the blood of my own kind I wiped out my disgrace. I did not object to the Buzzard that replaced the Dicky-bird. Though an offensive object to some, the Buzzard was to me an acceptable namesake.

"Aw, just one!"

It was Lee's cajoling voice. Beyond the fountain in the moonlit court which led to Jasmine's house, I could dimly see a white figure. Turning my head away sharply, I gave a smart ring at the doorbell. But I could not resist listening for her answer. My heart pounded disconcertingly. *I had never dared so far.*

Through the door that opened to my ring gushed a jet of light and laughter. While I answered greetings my eyes ran over the crowd that had come to the Gray's home to tell us good-bye. Yes, there they were at the back of the room . . . Lee and Jasmine. They had come in the portico entrance. As her eyes met mine I wondered—— how had she answered Lee?

"Right oh, every time," yelled Toby Christian jolting me out of a troubled trance. "You're stuck!"

"Stuck?" I repeated stupidly.

"We're guessing everybody that rings the bell," explained Betty Frost, wheeling about me as if she were a young gull and I a particularly choice crust thrown on the water. "Step—ring—that's a girl. Step—stop—ring—that's a boy. Boys have to take time to comb their tresses, you know. And every one we guess right has to do a stunt."

"Step—full stop—that's the Buzzard. It takes him longer than any one else to dress his feathers," Tony elaborated. "Come through with a stunt, my boy."

"Haven't much time for stunting."

I looked from the clock to Jasmine. Lee was on her heels. Through some unwritten code of my own I had expected him to give me the last few minutes of a whole evening with her. But Lee had an air of settled proprietorship. I cherished the suspicion of her secret preference for me, however—doubtless Lee entertained a similar one —and I meant to reap its benefits. What man has done man can do. I had as much nerve as Lee.

In the meantime the crowd was howling.

"Train or no train, you have to do your bit," announced Betty, once more putting on the gull and bread attraction.

"All right," said I, thinking fast. "Two fellows sit down here in the middle of the room— Toby, you'll do—and Lee—that's the dope—and we blindfold you. Then you wait till we get the show ready and you have to guess from the speeches what we're staging."

"What's the name of this stunt?" asked Lee uneasily from behind his bandage.

"It's called—Blind Man's Movies," I answered. "Come on, the rest of you—hurry up."

"The stunt is," I whispered outside, "to see how long those two goats will sit there."

I caught Jasmine by the hand and leaving the rest in suppressed laughter at sight of the solemn, trustful figures, I ran with her out into a corner of the court screened off by magnolias.

"We sure gave them the merry ha-ha," I chuckled.

She laughed, little rustles of leafy laughter. In the wavy moonlight I could just see her with the bloom on her skin, the round, soft firmness of a peach. Her eyes, too, held the tropical warmth of the ripening sun on an orchard and her hair was full of fruity tints. Even her hands were frail and twining like the young shoots on a tree. As I looked down at her I grew suddenly afraid.

"Well, goodbye, Jack," I said in a rigid voice.

"Good-bye, Dick," she answered.

Was this all? My heart beat quickly. No, I could never do it . . . I would wait till I came back . . . But that was a long time . . . I must do it now. I couldn't . . . Then unexpectedly a magnolia dipping in the breeze shuttered her face from the moonlight. In that kind darkness I groped for her soft lips with my own, groped and found them.

She was mine! The earth was mine! I was sure now what her answer had been to Lee. Poor old Lee! My heart sang in triumph at her first kiss.

"When I come back," I whispered uncertainly.

"Why do you go?" she asked slowly.

"Oh, I have to go!"

"But what do you have to go for?"

I looked down at her helplessly. She was a girl. She would never understand.

"Why, to see life—and get a pop at the Germans—and not be a quitter."

And that in chronological order was my creed. I did not know then how the values would shift.

She laughed softly, those little rustles of laughter.

"But when I come back——" I could not seem to finish.

She looked up at me in silence. Again I sought and found assurance on her lips.

Somewhere a clock stroked the midnight air with a touch of silver.

"I'll have to go now," I said and stood still. "But I'll write. And you write, won't you?"

She promised.

"I must go now," I repeated and still stood,

unable to leave her. At last I gave myself a jerk. With a last long kiss, I turned away.

"Say!" I shouted on the steps to the scattered couples. "We're not going to have time for that show, after all. Toddle along, Lee, and get your suitcase. Meet you at the station. No time to lose. Good-bye, everybody, good-bye—good-bye!"

There was a rush to the courtyard, a flutter of handkerchiefs, there were cries of farewell. With his bandage shoved back on his head, Lee shot a glance from me to Jasmine. I waved my hat and turned down the street.

In a moment I heard Lee's step behind me. I looked around. His serious face was flushed but he showed no sign of resentment. As he swung along beside me with the grace of a perfect animal I thought him unusually handsome. This added to my sense of triumph.

"Leave your bag at the station?" I asked mechanically. I was back under the magnolias.

"Just what I was going to tell you 'bout soon as I got my breath," he answered, speaking very fast. "Kid, I've been thinking it over and I believe we're fools to go to Orleans without any jack or any sure job. I believe we'd better stick around till we find out if there's a real thing waiting for us down there."

"After we've told every one good-bye?" I gasped. "Sneak back now like licked curs? Not on your life. Come on, old man, be a sport."

"Well," said Lee resolutely, "I've decided to wait till I have something to go on. But I tell you what. If you find there's jobs for both of us in New Orleans, wire me and I'll join you."

We were at the depot now. I stopped full under the light and looked at him, at the loose ends of his red mouth, at the hot dark eyes that always met mine with too steady a frankness.

"If you're yellow enough to back down now," I said, "you'll never hear from me again."

"Well, I can't see it your way," he answered stubbornly. "But good luck anyhow, old scout."

We shook hands and without waiting for me to jump on the train that had panted into the station, he left.

From the back platform I looked my last at home—the old Spanish town in the desert sleeping through the balmy winter night. After my hour of heady satisfaction came a moment of dismay. I was a little upset by Lee's shabbiness, a little hungry for another moonlit moment under the magnolias, a little desolated at thought of my mother listening in the quiet house to the roar of the train taking me away.

Scant time I had, however, for these emotions. I had expressed my bag straight through to New Orleans and bought my ticket only to the next station a few miles off. For with a fortune of just ten dollars I should have to steal the rest of the ride. So I hid in the blind till the train reached Houston. There I bought another ticket to the next station where I fell in with hobos who taught me to ride the rods.

At every stop we took on men who, like us, were beating their way East. They were the carrion of the labouring world. They were the men who picked up the refuse of industry, gathering canteloupes in Arizona, reaching Nebraska just in time to harvest grain, going on to Oregon in the autumn for the logging work. Now they were drifting down to New Orleans for the banana season.

I have wallowed in mud with human swine. I have tended cattle better kept than we who tended them. But I have never seen anything to compare with the filth of Marks' Yard in New Orleans.

Marks was contracting men to take over mules for the British Government. Bums all over the

country had read the advertisement that attracted
Lee. As a consequence there were hundreds of
us waiting for the promised jobs. Every man
that arrived was told that he would get work on
the next ship; pay was to be fifty dollars and a
return trip if he wanted it.

While we waited assignment we lived in the
Yard. Here Marks provided service in the form
of a huge kettle, an open fire and tin dippers.·
Board consisted of a soup-bone flung each morning into the kettle. If we wanted to elaborate
this stock, that was our own affair. As we invariably did, we detailed certain men every day
to get ingredients for the Mulligan. Some pulled
carrots from vegetable carts, some stole rice from
the rice mills. With a deference for nuances I,
who had beaten my way by train, refused to steal
food. I was therefore detailed to beg bread from
a bakery. This duty I performed with more industry because of a pretty Creole who tended
counter and gave me all the stale loaves I could
carry away.

Once a week the men emptied out the soup-
bone, stripped, put their shirts in the kettle and
had their boiling-up. After serving as tub the
versatile kettle was once more united with its
soup-bone. Fresh from my mother's ·ordered

household I was not yet acclimated to the dual personality of that kettle; and after the first boiling-up, avoiding the Mulligan, I spent the last of my ten dollars on beans and sinkers. For two days I could live on twenty-five cents. When my last quarter went I began unloading bananas on the docks. I could make a few cents a day over meals. Every time I found a banana too ripe to ship I slipped it into my pocket; or if I saw a whole ripe hand I threw it under a pile of straw to be divided in the Yard.

As every day I was expecting to sail I had no letters sent here; and since that triumphant moment under the magnolias I had not heard from Jasmine. But I wrote often to her, telling as much of my life as was expedient and planning for that indefinite time when I should come back, rich and distinguished, to reward her fidelity. Now I could write the words that I had dumbly tried to speak. But in spite of youthful arrogance I saw the humour of the situation. Still squeamish about the kettle, either for laundry or table use, I had not bathed since I left home. My clothes were greasy, my hair was unkempt. I was writing in a yard which would make an Indian camp look like a model of sanitation, among men who would make a siwash himself look as if he had just stepped from his valet's hands. And I smiled as I thought where my letters were going—to that dainty little beauty in the old Moorish house.

In the meantime two weeks had passed. Numerous ships had gone out. Every half a hundred men that went by boat left a hundred more coming in by train. And still Marks advertised. Why he wanted to supply soup to more men than he had to, I could not understand. When I got to England I learned how he paid himself a high rate of interest. For the present I was tired of waiting. So, armed with his letter and my passport, I went to register a kick at the British consulate. There I ran into Marks himself.

"Look here," I said, loud enough for the consul to hear, "I've got a letter from you promising me a job the day I get here. I've watched one boat after another off. What's the meaning of this?"

"Letter from me? Vy didn't you tell me, vy didn't you tell me? Take it to my foreman. He'll ship you at vonce," he answered, sliding me out of the consul's hearing.

Education, presence, impudence—whatever it was that enabled me in my greasy attire to attack Marks at the consul's office, I was grateful for it.

Out of several hundred men just as entitled as I to go, I was scheduled to sail next day.

Before it was light next morning the chosen forty were lined up on the dock. Our ship was the *Dunedin* from Leith. Our business was to take care of six hundred and thirty mules. These long-eared passengers were shown more consideration than we; for while we were kept waiting all day on the dock, they were shown at once to their staterooms by the coloured attendants.

After the last darky had run his mule down the chute there was nothing to amuse us. It was growing dusk. We had eaten nothing since morning. Just as we were getting so tired and hungry that brawls were breaking out all along the line, Marks bustled up.

Marks took his stand near the forward hatch and, too rapidly for any one to hear, read our articles. We were then shoved forward, a pen was thrust at us, and with Marks screaming at us to step lively and give the next fellow a chance, we wrote our signatures. We were in the dark, we were pushed forward, we were all terrified for fear we should miss our chance to go. Under these conditions no one tried to read his articles. For all I knew, I might have agreed to murder my mother and hand her jewels over to Marks.

It was six o'clock before we swung off. Our quarters were in the poop where pine bunks in tiers of two lined the walls. In the centre stood the eating tables. In one corner were the four faucets and basins that made up our toilet facilities.

Out of the forty men thirty of us were selected as muleteers. The other ten were more highly specialised—the veterinary and his assistant, the watchman, carpenter, first and second cook and four foremen. The personnel of the foremen was an Englishman, two ham actors with red socks and pink neckties, and the head foreman who had never missed a scrap of any size from the Boer War down. After one of these recreational bouts, when his nose had been bitten smoothly off his face, he was known as Puggy.

The foremen, I discovered as soon as I was on board, had armed themselves with clubs. As I began to recall stories of shanghai, my stomach gave way. Just then a fish-faced giant called Sockeye, ambling up to Puggy, stood looking down at him with his lips drawn back from his teeth in an attempt at an amiable smile.

"In the best naughtycal circles," he said softly, knocking the club out of Puggy's armpit, "gemman don't carry canes on shipboard. Awften and awften have I saw my friend Rockyfeller check his cane before starting a croose on his yawt, *The Kerosene Kan.*"

Sauntering over to the other foremen he collected their sticks and threw them overboard. Then he flashed upon his superiors a smile of benevolent ferocity that nailed them where they stood.

But now less lurid troubles concerned me. The Forty had all been behind bars. Arson, forgery, murder, vagrancy and vice at best—such, were their achievements. They were as proud of Sockeye's distinguished career in crime as a mother whose son lands in the Supreme Court. I was the only one in disgrace. I had never done time, I had never even been drunk, I had worked hard, and until now I had indulged a degenerate taste for bathing. Worst of all I was a minister's son.

I did my best to improve. I discarded the fork as effete and relied solely upon the virile knife as an aid to nourishment. Even had I not been forced to, I should have left off brushing my teeth. I dug up a crime or two for which I had escaped hanging only by desperate cunning. I would have jumped overboard sooner than have it known that any ancestor of mine had fallen so low as to affect a butler. I was just twenty, the youngest in the crowd, and I hoped for leniency because of youth. There was still time to turn over a new leaf. But in spite of my earnest desire to reform, the scent of the finger-bowl clung round me still. To my shame Sockeye branded me Percy.

As Percy then that first night I turned in to my bunk. I was fully dressed in overalls, boots, sweater and coat; for it had turned off bitter on the water, particularly after the warmth of New Orleans, and the sweating of the steel decks inside the poop intensified the cold.

When Puggy cursed us awake in the morning my face was raw. I had got a rash from the sack of hay that served as mattress and pillow. So after that, in spite of the increasing cold and the thin cotton blanket, I always took off my coat at night and spread it under my head. My best suit I kept in my bag in the locker under my bunk.

I was gingerly feeling the beefsteak I wore for a countenance that first morning when I saw Sockeye shaking the shoulder of Stiffy, the lumberjack snoring beside me.

"Algrenon," minced Sockeye, "draw Mastah Puhcy's bawth and lay out his little velvick soot."

"I hem Stiffy's sawmill runnin' the night

shift," put in one of the men as Stiffy's breathing sharpened from a rumble to a buzz.

"Yes, and cuttin' a mighty poor grade of timber, too," commented Sockeye, sinking a long, spare elbow in Stiffy's side.

I rolled to my feet. In a choppy sea the little tramp was bucking like a broncho, now pitching forward on her nose, now rearing back on her hind legs, then coming down stiff on all fours. It was the first time I had ever been on the ocean. I staggered to the table.

The "slum" of beef broth and hardtack left over from last night's supper was fried for breakfast. There was no coffee. But if I had sat down to chilled strawberries or hot waffles I couldn't have touched them. After one night the stench alone was enough to put a man off his food. I didn't need that rolling sea to make me fast.

The six hundred odd mules were quartered in the hold, crosswise, faces towards the inside of the ship, tails to the water. The stalls were so small that the keeper could not get in beside the mule; in fact they were too small for the mules to move. Each mule was tied to a headboard coming to his shoulders. To this was strapped a tin pan for his grain. Two quarts of oats, one of bran and all the hay he could eat was the daily ration. When we weren't carrying hay we were fetching water from the tanks at the end of the deck.

Three of us were assigned aft to thirty mules —Snake, the half-breed, Chuck and myself.

"Get out, you lily-livered sons of corpses, and feed them mules," Puggy rallied us that first morning as we rose distastefully from the fried slum.

"Mastah Puhcy's appetite has been delicate of late," simpered Sockeye, twisting an imaginary bracelet on his hairy wrist. "His papa and me took him to see Dr. Bigbugs, the most ixpensive pheezishun in Noo York, and the doctor said a sea voyage would do him a *world* of good. Run out now, Puhcy, and breathe the oozone."

Had I not been otherwise engaged I should have suffered under Sockeye's affronts. But imagine a first attack of sea-sickness. Imagine it magnified by filthy food, filthy men, filthy quarters. Imagine climbing over steam-pipes and bales of hay or scrambling up and down ladders, a pail of water or a measure of grain in each hand. Imagine that the mules were as sick as you and no respecters of persons. Twelve hours of it with no surcease. Twelve hours of tossing, deathly sick and sleepless, on my bunk. Then another day when I was too sick to bear the sight of food, when I stag-

gered up and down the deck, across the steam-
pipes, over bales of hay, a bucket in each hand—
up and down, up and down. No wonder Sockeye's taunts failed to draw blood. I was no longer
a being with sensibilities. I was a contrivance for
feeding mules. I ticked off only two emotions.
One was the determination to stay on the job.
The other was a hunger for cleanliness and women
and affection. I was sick for my mother and for
Jasmine, a sickness that absorbed and dilated with
bodily pain.

But while rough seas rolled through the scrip-
tural span, at the end of the third day a dove of
peace descended upon me. And I say with pride
that although I had neither eaten nor slept during
that time, not one of my charges missed a grain
of his oats or ever suffered for water.

The poor mules! We had now struck the
northern cold and some of them died of conges-
tion of the lungs. The rest were shivering and
seasick and angry. To keep them from breaking
their halters we had to tie their heads fast with
ropes, soaked in oakum so they would not eat
them. We had also to fasten them so tight that
they could not chew each other's necks.

The seas were running clear over the boat at
times. The winds were so bitter that the upper

deck where I worked was slippery with sleet. It was no easy thing to keep my footing on those glassy slopes over which I slid with the water buckets, back and forth, a hundred times a day. I was glad therefore when I was transferred to the lower hold where I had at least the protection of the deck. Here I took care of fifty mules with Shorty, a pigmy of six feet six. The two of us cleaned up our work as well as we could but we were short-handed. This I remedied unexpectedly along with another disturbance.

"We're off the Banks," announced Puggy one morning at slum. Some one began to whistle "Banks and Braes."

"Yep," repeated Puggy, with a wave of his hand to the north, "the Banks is over there."

I waved *my* hand towards the mules.

"The Brays," I ventured, "are down there."

"Haw, haw!" guffawed the foreman.

Encouraged by his good humour I seized the moment to ask a favour.

"Puggy, Shorty and I have too much work."

"All right," said Peggy, "you can have Monny. He's no good anyhow."

When we arose from slum I attempted to claim my treasure.

"I need Monny myself, Miss Percy," announced Red, one of the ham actors with the scarlet hose. As if that settled it, he turned away.

"Puggy said we could have Monny," I protested.

"Close your baby face, Perce, or I'll slap it up to a peak and knock the peak off."

"It would take a man to do that," I retorted loftily.

I had tried to prove by the way I handled my work that Percy was a misnomer. I had not succeeded. Now though my knees wobbled I was thirsting for a fight.

With a grunt Red jumped me. I was five feet eleven to his six feet, and was some twenty pounds lighter. I was wiry but my muscles had not yet cemented.

His left went up for a guard, his right shot for my jaw.

"Red's beatin' up Percy!" shouted Shorty to the crowd of muleteers scattering to their various posts. "Red's beatin' up Percy!"

Even as I jerked my head, even as Red's fist glanced my jaw, I could hear the cries swell into a roar: "Red's beatin' up Percy!"

As far as brute strength goes he could have mangled me. My chief asset was a clear head. As I feinted with my left I landed with the right. I had caught him behind the ear. He went down flat. Then I heard the roar changing to: "Percy's beat up Red! Percy's beat up Red!"

Red got to his feet just in time to meet Sockeye's terrifying smile as he said in the caressing tone reserved for putting foremen in their place:

"You old stewbum, you dish of slumgullion, if you ever touch that kid again I'll—I'll—his voice grew softer and more terrible—"I'll eat you up! The way he stuck to them mules, tendin' them like a mother and him sick as one of them hisself with you rottin' in your bunk! I'll eat you up!"

He wheeled about, shoved aside the men who were shaking my hand and gave me a whack on the back that sent me spinning.

I have been decorated since then by the French government. But never have I felt such pride as thrilled through me with the realisation that at last I was a member in good standing with the Forty. Percy I remained but Percy was no longer a badge of shame. It was a term of endearment. And Sockeye, who had first fastened it to me, now invited me to go buddy with him!

This fellowship shortened the rest of the trip. We used to sit about the stove in the poop at night playing blackjack, listening to Sockeye's intimate

babble of J. Pierp, John D. and Andy C., or singing "barber harmony."

There were not only many good natural voices
among the men but a few finely trained ones—
voices that had been heard in light opera or church
choirs before their owners had become outcast.
"Going Down the River," "Tipperary," which had
just hit America hard, and "Oh, Eveline" were
among the favourites. Then there were ribald
songs I do not dare name, songs known to every
hobo from Mobile to Missoula. But the selection
that impressed me most was still another.

Whenever I hear "Abide With Me" I see two
pictures. The first is in the little church at home.
I see a weeping congregation—the widow of the
sexton, the greaser vendor of tamales, the com-
mander of the fort, the tall, spare banker, Jase-
mine Gray, my eyes seeking hers for comfort—
all who had come within touch of my father's loving spirit. I see my mother, tragic in her tearless-
ness. I see the bishop as he repeats the solemn
conviction that the flesh is futile and only the soul
triumphant. I see my father's figure in the flower-
heaped casket and the gentle face dimmed of all
expression now save for a thirsty look as if he were
drinking rest. Then from the choir loft I hear

four voices breaking as they sing "Abide With Me."

The second picture is in the poop on the mule ship. Around the red quivering stove men lie on bunks, on tables, on the floor. Such men! Whiskered and ragged, the foul odours of their bodies mingled with the foul odours of the ship, the stale fumes of food, the reek of bad tobacco. Even through their obscene ditties the emotional appeal of music reaches them. The same appeal in popular hits or church hymns, it lifts them to something higher. From coarse ballads to ragtime, from ragtime to sacred music they pass. Evil of mind, vile of tongue, selfish and slothful and ruthless as wolves, for the moment and for the moment only a softer feeling possesses them—a feeling for home, for women, for some strange God of their own. Sockeye's melting tenor soars above the rest. And forty voices chant in four-part harmony "Abide With Me."

Another and more sordid pastime for those evenings about the stove was known as reading the news. Then would the men peel off their shirts and diligently search for "crumbs" as the greybacks were called. Reading the news was practically the only attempt at cleanliness. The water was so bad that it was less filthy to go dirty than try to be clean. During the three weeks on board I washed my face just six times.

Drinking water was almost as offensive as washing water. We drank from the mule-tanks which were filled with the mud of the Mississippi River. Food was even worse. We lived on rotten tinned beef that was boiled at noon, fried at night for hash and fried over with hardtack for breakfast. There was neither coffee nor bread. There was however a ton or more of carrots for the mules. The carrots rotted and during our leisure moments Shorty, Monny and I had to cut away the decayed spots so that the remainder could be served to us.

"Anything our long-faced friends don't want we'se welcome to," Monny expressed it.

The routine of the carrot was the same as that of canned beef—boiled at noon, fried at night, fried again for breakfast. After a few months of service at the front a man is not fussy about his food. But it's all I can do now to sit at the same table with a carrot.

"You're not much of a student," my mother used to say grudgingly. "But you seem to have a gift for the way out."

I found the way out now.

The officers on deck of course had much better

meals than ours. Among other luxuries they ate bread every day. I enjoyed a calling acquaintance with Slim, the cook. And one evening I sauntered up to watch him at his baking which had to be done at night. The smell of fresh bread tantalised me unbearably.

"It must be hard to work all night," I commented.

"Damned hard."

"Don't you almost go to sleep?"

"Droppin' in my tracks this minnit."

"I'll bake your bread if you want to put over a nap," I suggested. "Used to be a baker myself."

Slim looked at me suspiciously but I told him enough to convince him that I knew how to bake. Off he went and slept for three hours.

"Can I have a piece of bread?" I asked when he returned.

"Sure," said he hospitably.

He broke off a thick chunk which I ate as only an American can who has not touched bread for two weeks.

The next night I offered myself again.

"Ye don't need to wait till I git back for that there hunk of bread," he said expansively as he went off to his nap.

I didn't stop at bread. Among the officers' rations I found some sacks of potatoes and onions. Slipping out a few of each I fried them over Slim's stove. By the time he caught me we were such good friends that he never saw me when I prepared my nightly supper of hot lyonnaise potatoes.

By stealing next from the mules and the coolie crew I supplemented the fare for the whole Forty. I discovered that the crew of Chinks had refused to work without a special bread of Chinese fish. There were sacks of these dried fish in the galley and every night I pulled a few out by their tails to drag back to our cabin. Then filling one of the mule buckets half way up with water and a handful of the rock salt that belonged to the animals, I set it on the stove. When it came to a boil I poured in some meal also filched from the donkeys. This would cook up to a brimming bucket of hot oatmeal which we ate with chunks of dried fish.

"The more mule fodder we eat the less our long-faced friends will founder," said Monny philanthropically, slipping hot porridge down his throat.

Thanks to this intervention none of the mules did founder. But Sally did worse.

Sally had red hair and the disposition that goes

with it. Any devilment she could execute was never too much trouble for Sally.

"Sally got a cold in her head last night," I said one morning to the vet.

"Sally would," was all the sympathy extended either to Sally or her keeper.

"Why don't you sponge out her nostrils with warm water and creosote?" asked Shorty.

"Why don't I brush a hyena's teeth?" retorted I.

Nevertheless I undertook the delicate operation of spraying Sally's aquiline nose. Shorty stood by with words of comfort and advice.

Sally made a few preliminary expostulations. She made them resonantly but ineffectually. She then opened the real debate with the good old feminine argument of biting. I rebutted by slamming her over the head with a bucket.

> "Be gentle with your little boy
> Beat him when he sneezes;
> He only does it to annoy
> Because he knows it teases."

Shorty was singing. Even at this intense moment I wondered how Shorty happened to be familiar with this nonsense classic—perhaps it had been quoted in some musical comedy. But I could waste only a second on Shorty's pursuits. For Sally advanced a powerful *a priori* argument, followed it by a smashing *a fortiori*, dealt a few scattering but well-chosen kicks and closed the debate by an irrefutable argument with her head that left her opponent no ground to stand upon. The debate was unanimously adjudged in favour of the negative.

"Rope her head," shouted Shorty as I picked myself up and out of the way of the dancing Sally. "You gotta handle her as if she was a woman. Rope her head!"

"Stroke her ears if you're that intimate with her," I snarled, caressing my arm from which Sally had neatly clipped a piece.

"Give me the rope, you poor fish," said Shorty. "Now, you little she-devil, you little hellion"— he looked masterfully in her eye—"I'll learn you to——"

Six feet six of Shorty lay on the deck. Sally stood on top of him. She had turned a somersault over the headboard to which she was still tied! Her neck was twisted like a rope, her head was held in a vice against the outside of the board, but her figure was erect. Her tail waved breezily over Shorty's prostrate form. The feat would have broken any one's neck but Sally's.

It took half a dozen of us to lift her off, stand her on her head till we could untwist her neck and hold her while the vet, who felt at last that here was a patient worthy his professional interest, washed out her nostrils.

Sally had one unswerving admirer on board and only one. This was Pete, the big grey mule who stood beside her. Like many giants, Pete, who knew no fear before any one his own size and sex, was completely subjugated by the little minx. So enchanted was he with her dash and spirit that he even gave her his hay. With doglike devotion in his eyes he would push it over to her. Would Sally then bray: "You keep it, Pete," or "Thank you, I *will* have a little more if you can spare it"? No, without a word of thanks Sally would dispose of the hay, snapping between bites at Peter who seemed grateful even for this attention. If Sally had been a biped she would have belonged to that class of women who say: "You can't treat a husband like a human being." And she'd have married some big brute who would have stood for her, just as Pete did. I often wondered, had Pete asserted himself, if Sally wouldn't have given him a better deal. The only time he ever did I thought I saw a glint of admiration in her eye.

This was the morning we ran up the harbour of

Dublin. We had been ordered to discharge the mules. To a man we refused. Running mules into a chute was a darky's job. Besides we were within reach of land and brimming with spirits. Here too was a chance to get even with the ship-master for the dirty deal he had handed us, here when it was too late for him to retaliate. And when the captain realised that we were not going to unload those mules he sent for a company of raw Irish recruits fresh from the bogs on their way to the front.

The mules, as I have said, were boxed so closely that they could scarcely move. As our contract called for cleaning them we led them one at a time out on deck and scraped them off as well as we could. This was not very well and when they were run on shore at Dublin they were still thickly caked with manure and New Orleans mud. Lounging about the dock, we enjoyed the struggles of the Irish with the shaggy beasts.

A darky fulfils all the yearnings of the mulish heart. The Irish on the contrary lacked not only a native affinity but experience as well. They had never even seen a mule. Any darky knows that a mule can not be led. But here was a small bog-trotter trying to lead three at once across the drawbridge.

One of the three was Pete. While his two companions pulled for opposing shores Pete stood firm. His four feet, spread apart, seemed driven into the dock. His peaceful eye was half closed.

Pat dropped the other two ropes and applied himself to Pete. Tall and grey and rock-ribbed as a mountain Pete paid no more attention to him than if he were a mosquito.

"They're desert canaries—put salt on their tails and hear 'em sing," called out one of our wits.

"Get behind and push," suggested another.

This advice appealed to Pat as more practical. He trustingly obeyed.

Without opening his sunny eye Pete doubled his right hind leg. Pat hurtled through the air like a baseball. Then not deigning to glance behind him the desert canary threw back his head, lifted his voice—such a voice as had never before been heard in Dublin—and singing passionately raced back and forth across the drawbridge. It was as if Gibraltar, tired of its reputation for steadiness, had gone vigorously to sowing its wild oats.

Men and mules cleared the path. All but Sally who did not move. It was evident that she expected Pete to get out of her way. But Pete neither swerved nor slackened. When he was within a foot of her Sally gave one bound with as much dignity as her health would allow. Whether her music loving soul vibrated to that ringing voice; whether, herself an artist at the hoof, she admired his technique; whether she suspected that Pete was more of a rake than she had given him credit for —I don't know. But as she moved out of reach of those compelling legs she flung him a glance over her shoulder. There was a softened look in her eye and her ears twitched meltingly.

By this time I was feeling sorry for Pat. So when Pete drew up with the air of a Caruso taking his curtain call, I jumped on his back and rode him over the drawbridge. The other mules of course followed. Pat and his compatriots were stunned by this simple method.

"The next bit on our programme, gentlemen," barked Monny, seeing their open-mouthed admiration, "will be by Percy, the Donk's Delight!"

When I again saw the American ponies, as the Irish called them, they were doing heroic service at the front. Upon renewing my acquaintance with them I learned that they had risen from the "Maude" of American song to the more patrician title of Percy. I often wondered if the honour were mine!

"Kept this open to give you my impressions of Dublin," I wrote that afternoon on the letter I had been composing to Jasmine all the way across. "So far they consist of heads and feet. The cops, whales to begin with, have spikes on their helmets that make them look about seven feet six. 'Pipe the size of the bull,' was all the men could say as we landed. Fortunately every cop we've seen so far has a brother on the New York police force which makes him adopt all Americans into the bosom of his family. And as for feet—well, I haven't seen a pair of shoes in Dublin that weren't shined. No matter how poorly dressed, how ragged or dirty a man is his boots are polished as an egg.

"I set sail with the fortune of one dollar that I had amassed loading bananas. It was still intact this morning; so in order to absorb local colour I set up a couple of the boys to Guiness' Stout and a box of Pell Mells. (N. B. Observe pronunciation.) After this debauch I had just a sixpence left and Puggy borrowed that. I was so flattered at having a sixpence to lend a foreman that I didn't mind the financial reverse. Not till afterwards did I remember that I had to get postage for this letter from that sixpence. Well, I'm a bold financier and I'll raise that two cents if I have to sell my boots. When Puggy saw my pride in giving him a sixpence he said graciously, 'That's a good pair of kicks you got there, Perce—I might wear them up town.' This suggestion has been made by every man on board. But I cling to those boots as a monk to his immortal soul—pun' not intended. They're my one valuable possession and I'm saving them against the time when I'm strapped—I mean when I'm on my uppers. (This letter looks all broken out with puns but they are *not* intentional.) Anyway nothing short of a stamp for this letter shall wring those boots from me.".

The boots were preserved to meet the need I had expected. The postage came through another channel.

Following a crowd of our men up a street I saw Black and Chuck disappear. From their hang-dog look I suspected a crooked deal and sauntered after them. I watched them go down under a little bridge where they met another man apparently by appointment. I edged along till I was close enough to see Chuck handling a curry-comb. Ready to put up any kind of a bluff to make two cents I yelled, "Hey, Chuck, what you doing with my curry-comb?"

"Who said this was your comb?" asked Chuck, jumping around like a startled rabbit.

"I said so," I answered noisily.

"Howdju know it's your comb?"

"How'd I know?"

At this delicate question I caught sight of the letter P cut into the back. I recognised it at once as Puggy's.

"Don't you know the alphabet yet?" I demanded angrily. "There's P for Percy."

"Well, I guess you caught me with the goods, Perce," Chuck conceded. "We was just disposin' of a few things to this here gentleman. He runs a liver stable."

"Of course if the liver stable gentleman wants this comb," I said, "I'll let it go for sixpence."

The gentleman took it at my price. He took also about a dozen other combs and brushes the two men had tucked in their pockets. I bought some stamps. As I mailed mother's letter and put Jasmine's in my pocket for a last postscript, I wondered what those two women would think if they knew my arrival on foreign soil was announced by means of a stolen curry-comb. Again my sense of honour had made concession; I would not steal carrots from a vegetable cart but I would sell a curry-comb from the *Dunedin!* Seeing this act through my mother's eyes, I found it taking on an ugly aspect; and I resolved to drift into no more easy little thefts. My remorse was not shared by the others who were so sore at the treatment we had received on a British transport that they declared anything they could filch from any one in the British Isles would be just retribution. And it was in pursuit of this policy that, when I went into a shop to buy postals with my remaining two cents, half a dozen mule-skinners attended me. It was not till later that I knew why. They came out richer by several dollars worth of pens, paper and pencils. The same principle of sabotage was applied to a restaurant where the boys set up ham and eggs with the proceeds of the curry-combs; and where, in spite of my protests, salts, peppers, spoons, even vinegar-cruets were rapidly disappearing.

"If you wanna kiss the hand that feeds you slum, all right, Miss Percy," said Black, when a tobacco-shop was next threatened by our patronage. "Here's a sixpence. Go as far as you like."

The gleam of unnatural goodness in his eye was not belied. While I bought cigarettes with the sixpence, a quiet but effectual activity prevailed among my friends. Snake, who had stowed away a big tin of cigarettes, was following it with a mate when Whitey, who had no pockets, attempted to help him to a third. The two tins banged together. The girl behind the counter looked up sharply.

"Give me back those cigarettes," she cried.

There were loud protestations. Outraged honesty was in every voice.

"I'll call an officer," she threatened, planting herself in the doorway.

It was a disconcerting moment. Snake dared not pull out one tin for fear it would disgorge others. Disclosures by an officer would be equally embarrassing.

The girl put her hand on a bell. Just then Williams stepped forward.

"One moment, madam," said he, flashing his gold teeth upon her. "What are you talking about?"

"Those two men stole a tin of cigarettes," she answered, "and I'm going to have an officer in."

"Well, if those two poor fellows who have been doing military service for your country, madam——"

"He means mulitary service," whispered Sockeye to me.

"——If they want a little thing like a box of cigarettes, they shall have it. I'll pay for it myself."

He threw down the price of one tin.

"Now, gentlemen, is there anything else I can get to show my respect for you?"

The gentlemen modestly disclaimed further testimonial. This restraint met its own reward. Taking stock a safe distance away, we estimated that we had repaid ourselves for service to the British government by at least fifteen dollars' worth of pipes and tobacco.

Thus buttressed with smokes, we set out in a body that night to see Dublin. "Where's the main stem?" was the chorus that greeted every policeman. I dropped behind to mail my letter to Jasmine. Then guided by the noise in a nearby saloon, I pushed open the door. The reflection in the mirror on the opposite wall gave me the first sight of myself. My sweater and overalls had some time ago become fodder for Sally. I was now protruding from a Salvation Army costume that Puggy had traded for my fountain pen. Through the hat that Puggy had lavishly thrown in, my hair pushed up in ambitious bunches.

My companions were equally arresting. Monny shrank far into the recesses of a suit he had purchased from Sockeye. Shorty, like Marco Bozzaris, was bursting at every vein of the frock coat he had picked up at a rummage sale. Stiffy, the most sustained in attire, wore a lumberman's shirt and corduroys. Hoggy, the second cook, had once been a bandsman; now in his faded livery of maroon and black he sat playing the piano while Chuck, in a blanket coat and chaps, passed the hat. The proceeds were to go for drinks.

Inspired to provide a tobacco fund, I composed an Indian dance. It consisted of running back and forth on my haunches, singing, "Icta, mika, tiki, close ole cloochman." This I punctuated with a sturdy yelp by way of war-whoop, which confirmed my audience in its hope that America is peopled largely by savages. My gate receipts, as a consequence, were heavy.

Through its mysterious channels the whole night-world of Dublin had heard of our arrival. We left not a saloon unturned; and all the gamblers and thugs in the city, I think, were on our trail. So, too, were those other denizens of the underworld. Moths of the street, painted and haggard and gay, drawn by the new arrivals, I watched them swirling and eddying to the gaslight.

We were passing a station on our way to the ship when I saw something I never forgot. The memory of it came back when I needed it most, came again and again until it became a part of me. It was a carload of wounded men on their way home from some place in England where they had been fitted with artificial arms and legs. I have never felt more joy in my vitality than those crippled men felt in their pitiful substitutes.

As I saw the glow in those spent faces, reverence for what they had endured deepened into awe for what they now felt. Maimed, disabled, robbed in youth of youth's fleetness—how could they still be so happy? Not for long months was I to know the secret of that look. Now as I took off my hat it was in tribute to the merriment I could not understand.

Still bare-headed, I was looking after those joyous survivors—joking, chattering—when some distance behind the others came a man in a wheelchair. I stared at him first. He was young and romantically good-looking. Long suffering had not dimmed those sea-blue eyes nor that vigorous curve of profile. Like Phaëthon he seemed to have plunged straight into this street—straight to an earth he would never tread again. The handsome, untouched face, the broken body—just then it was I lifted my eyes to the woman wheeling his chair. At this moment Sockeye, who had been standing beside me, lurched forward and accidentally jostled the chair.

"Beast!" I heard the girl whisper it with such

a passion of scorn that even Sockeye jerked off
his hat. Unplacated she looked after him. Then
her eyes, moving back, chanced to meet my own.
In an instant the fierce resentment for her charge
changed to a swift curiosity, so fresh, so frank, so
impersonal that for the first time I remembered
how I looked. I gave a pull to my mere dialect of
a suit. She caught me doing it and a sudden
merry smile that had in it no whit of unkindness
brought an answer to my own eyes.

Long after she was gone I felt the something
invigorating in that quick, interested scrutiny.
With an imbecile smile at the recollection I started
off in my sieve of a cap and my Salvation Army
suit. That brief look of ours—it had been youth
asking of youth. Then as I walked on through the
Dublin streets I recalled what that glance of hers
had interrupted—the fierce protection in her Irish
eyes for the soldier in her charge. I stopped short.
For the first time I did not take for granted my
youth and my vigour and the world's answer to
these.

"God!" I said. "I'm glad I don't have to be
just pitied by a girl like that!"

CHAPTER II

A S I stepped from Paddington Station into London I came to a full stop in the middle of the street. A curse from a cabby made me look up. At the cabby's bitter scowl I smiled unresentfully. It was the first hansom I had ever seen that had almost run over me. But that was not what had pulled me up so short. It was the import of the words I had caught myself humming:

> "When I am dying
> Lean over me
> Softly, tenderly as the yellow roses droop in
>   in the wind from the south . . ."

The girl back in Dublin bending over the soldier with that passion of maternity—she had recalled it. It was one of Jasmine's songs. Sentimental even for my condition, it used to make me writhe to hear it in public. I used to squirm particularly over the last line—"the touch of your lips on my mouth." Now with a shame-faced laugh at my-

self for humming it, I began my search for lodgings.

It had taken me a week to get from Dublin to
London. Marks had promised to pay us off at
Dublin. But at Dublin we learned that we must
first clean the ship and take it to Berry Docks.
We toiled like Turks to clean that filthy ship;
and when we reached Berry Docks the shipmaster
said that as he was discharging the coolie crew we
must take the ship home. Then we would be paid
off in New Orleans.

Take the ship home? Never, we roared. Then
Williams because of his gold teeth and I because
of a clean collar were selected to protest to the captain. Neither of these arguments dazzled that
phlegmatic gentleman.

"You signed articles to bring the ship back—
what's the matter with you fellows?" he growled.

To our astonishment he produced the articles.
It was true. Marks had skipped one clause when
he read the document aloud; we had not been
given time to read it for ourselves.

"All right, sir," said I to the captain, who had
turned an insolent back, "I'll not sit down under
this dirty deal. I'll expose your little game."

"Well, I guess you know our names," he answered easily. A penniless scarecrow in a strange land held no terrors for him.

Tying about my neck my logging boots and my bag of good clothes which I had managed to keep intact under my berth, I jumped overboard and swam ashore. The time had come to part from my boots. Changing into my best suit, I hunted a cobbler. The cobbler was less susceptible to the charms of those boots than the mule-skinners had been; so although I had paid twenty dollars for them I was glad to sell them for sixty cents. This was the price of a round-trip to Cardiff, where the American consul lived.

The consul, too, was indifferent; but after I had threatened to report him at home for refusal to help an American in distress, he gave me a letter to the skipper demanding my discharge. So the skipper had to pay me off—thirteen dollars and sixty-five cents. This was the remnant of my wage. Marks had deducted Ritz-Carlton prices for board that couldn't be eaten, mouldy tobacco, and soap we never had a chance to use. I knew now why he had kept us on the dock: the board bill we were rolling up for that dirty soup-bone was to be deducted from our pay. Then he sold rotten overalls and paper-soled shoes to all the men who would buy; the ninety per cent profit for this haberdashery was also deducted from our pay. And next, hired by the British government to deliver mules in Dublin, he saved the expense of a crew on the return voyage by misreading the articles and refusing pay till we had brought the ship home. A financial genius was Marks!

Most of the gang had no ambition beyond a few dollars for drinks; and on condition that they receive half-pay now they agreed to take the ship home. I, as is usual in such cases, was too eager to get away to bother with reporting the crooked game to the British government as I should have done. So I left the men crazy with whiskey, beating up the town—left my particular pals with a regret that surprised me. After all they were my only friends within a thousand miles. And I had heard nothing from home. I had first ordered my mail sent to Paris. Then deciding to enlist in the British army I had written to Paris asking the American Express there to send my mail to the London office. My one comfort during this month of sordid hardship had been hope of the letters piling up for me in England—letters from mother and the boys and one letter the very thought of which made my heart beat faster.

Had it not been Sunday then when I reached London I should have gone straight to the American Express. But one more night must pass. And highhearted with the hopes of to-morrow and the stir of the first great city I had ever seen I entered a tobacco shop.

I had now just ten dollars. I could not consider a hotel, so as I bought a postal for Jasmine I asked the shopgirl to direct me to lodgings. With a quick flirt of her lashes she looked me over. I had not bathed since I left home and until I reached Paris I bore a faint mulish scent. But my best suit evidently gave me a veneer of respectability, for one night in the part of town to which she sent me would be my financial ruin.

"Hol-ee cats, this is no place for Percy," thought I, dismayed by the grandeur of the hotels.

I started off in an opposite direction and walked until it was too dark to see the houses. Then, finding a bobby with a goodnatured face, I asked him to direct me to a cheap hotel.

"My woman can put you up for the night," he answered tentatively.

I jumped at the suggestion. He gave me his address. But as I lifted the knocker on his door I remembered that I did not know his name.

"Is this the lady of the house?" I asked the woman who answered the knock.

She stared at me silently. She was a big-jowled

THE SWALLOW 51

woman with a figure that doubled in at the waist.

"Is this the lady of the house?" I repeated.

Her mouth dropped open but she only continued to stare with bovine eyes from under heavy, hornlike brows.

"I met an officer who directed me here to find a room," I explained, disconcerted by her silence. "He didn't tell me his name."

"Oh! Eh! That's it, is it? You can have the room then."

She took me up to a tiny stall of a room. As she lit the gas she added impressively:

"But I ign't no lydy. I'm *Mrs*. White."

When the bobby returned that night I heard her telling him about my strange question. In fact during my whole stay she never recovered from my unconscious flattery. The joke became a family institution.

"And I says to him," I would hear Mrs. White repeating, "I says, 'But I ign't Lydy White. Me husband's not come into the title *yet*.' "

Next morning after swallowing a bun and glass of milk in a neighbouring tea-room I walked to the American Express. As I demanded my mail my breath quickened. I was wondering how Jasmine would begin her letter.

"If you don't hurry," I said behind my teeth

to the clerk who sifted the letters with monstrous calm, "I'll choke to death before your eyes."

"No, sir, nothing here," he said, wheeling about as if in answer to my threat.

"You haven't the name right then—Byrd," I said sharply. "Look again, please."

Turning wearily on his heel he went again through the pigeon-hole.

"No, sir, no mail for Byrd."

I stared at the sleek-haired, sleek-eyed young man whose level gaze met mine uncaringly. Then I walked out. There was an ache in my throat.

After one stunned moment I felt I must do something violent. I started to run. I stopped in the arms of an officer.

"After all," I said to him, "this is wartime. Mails are slow. The letter will be here soon."

The bobby gave me one disgusted look. I backed off from that impregnable blue front.

"You must be in a bad way, young sir. Be off about your business," said he.

"You'd be in a bad way too," thought I, "if the dearest little girl in the world hadn't written you for a month."

But taking his advice I walked briskly off to the American consulate.

"What do you want?" inquired a young squirt

behind the desk to one of my countrymen ahead of me.

"I'm broke. I want to get home."

"Better stay here and help out if you're broke. Plenty of work here. What do *you* want?"

Having thus helpfully disposed of the man in front he was addressing himself to me.

"I want to get into the war. What steps shall I take?"

"Take the next ship home. What are *you* doing here?"

He leaned over to the man behind me but I planted myself squarely under his nose.

"*You* have a discontented disposition," I said. "Apparently no one can suit you. Now I'll not take any ship home until I have got into this war."

I flung myself out and down to the town hall in Chelsea.

"I want to enlist," I announced there.

As when leaving America, I gave my age as twenty-one. That was satisfactory. I gave my qualifications. They were satisfactory. Then I gave my birthplace.

"Oh! American! We can't use *you!*"

How many times I heard those words, always with the same scornful emphasis! From one recruiting office to another I went. Every few squares I was stopped by recruiting officers. Everywhere I saw signs, "Enlist Now! Help the Boys Over There!" Yet the feeling against America was so bitter that, needing men as she did, England would not use me.

"What have you got against America anyway?" I asked one recruiter who like the rest had lost interest at the mention of my nationality.

"When Belgium was violated *we* came to the rescue for honour's sake," he said melodramatically. "Why didn't you?"

> *"I came in, I came in, I came in,*
> *I came in to save my skin."*

I sang it into his face. "When our skins are in danger," I added, "we'll come in, too."

"Well," he called after me, "if you want to fight so much why don't you forget that you're an American? Then the King will too."

"To hell with the King and England," I retorted, "I'll never forget that I'm an American."

It was now evident that I should never get into the British army. By this time my money was almost gone. My only chance was to earn the price of a ticket to Paris and there pick up some kind of work till I could speak enough French to enlist in the French army.

I had supposed that with the labour shortage in England it would be easy to find work. Yet I tried every conceivable line. I applied for jobs as mechanic, chauffeur, baker. With a working knowledge of Spanish I tried to find a place as interpreter. I would have swept crossings or sold ribbons. But in commerce as in the army my nationality closed all doors to me.

Nevertheless I never appreciated America as I did then. For at home any man, any where, can get some kind of. work. But in England, young, strong, energetic as I was, I was actually facing starvation. It was unbelievable. It was grotesque. It was ghastly.

I reduced my eating expense to two cents a day. This sum would buy a cup of strong tea and a bun which I took at ten in the morning. Sometimes the waitress would slip me a second cup of tea.

As for my clothes, the feet of my socks were completely gone and I tied what was left around my ankles so carefully that I seemed to be hosed. The soles of my shoes, too, were gone and to keep my bare feet off the ground I fitted cardboard inside the uppers. In a large stock of clean collars lay my salvation. A fresh collar each morning with a fairly well-tailored suit gave me that valuable aid to success, a look of prosperity.

Every day and all day I tramped that grey, gaunt city. But no matter how far I walked, how aching my feet, I went each afternoon to the American Express for the mail that did not come. I was uneasy, harassed, stung. Even in wartime I should have heard from home by now.

On the fifth day of my tea and cake régime I discarded my birthplace and adopted the English tongue. With what was meant to be a broad Yorkshire accent I applied at Harrid's, Ltd., which, patterned after the American department store, was one of the largest stores in England. I had just come up from the country, I said, where I had managed my father's shop. Mr. White I gave for reference. That thrifty soul, his kindness, no doubt, given more elasticity by the fact that my rent was due, agreed to lie for me. On the strength of this fiction, the very Saturday I had reached my last cent, I landed a job as time-keeper. And on the strength of this job Mrs. White, trusting me till payday for my room, invited me to celebrate at Sunday breakfast in a pork pie.

I longed to say, "Make it to-night." Instead, to keep down the pangs of hunger, I went to bed. As I lay there from Saturday noon till Sunday morning I dreamed of one thing. Like a small-town youth who lets his imagination play about some girl coming for a summer visit, and who falls in love with the image he has created, my imagination played about that pork pie. I dwelt upon its size, its complexion, its inner nature. I hoped it would be large enough. I wondered how many helpings I might decently have.

It was large. It was thick. It was rich and indigestible, but Mrs. White apologised for its simplicity.

"Plain Yorkshire fare, sir," she said, while my famished eye followed her knife skirting the crust for an opportune opening. At last the knife plunged. A spoon followed to catch the juice. In a second my plate was heaped with meat and thick brown pastry. Beside it stood a huge cup of steaming coffee.

Three times I cleaned my plate and drained my cup. Three times they were filled again; the supply seemed inexhaustible. Each time I feared to risk a protest. Even Mrs. White's pleasure in my appreciation of her cookery might fail before my appetite did. But if the supply proved endless the demand did not. The time came when I could eat no more. Then the bobby, his weathered neck rolling over his Sunday collar, proffered me a long black cigar. With our feet on the fender of the open fire we sat silently smoking and recalling the charms of pork pie.

"That's the first real meal I've had since I left home," I said to Mrs. White when I finally rose to go. "I'm sure I never enjoyed one so much."

Tears sprang to her eyes.

"I only wish," she said, "that some French lady would feed pork pie to my own poor lad in the trenches. He relished it from his cradle, sir, and it reminded me of him to see you eat."

Next morning I went to work. My pay from Harrid's was twenty-five shillings a week "all found." This meant with free meals. Fortunately for me the company considered it good business to keep a restaurant for their employés. Otherwise I should have had to starve till my first pay day.

These meals at the store were solid and wholesome. Breakfast consisted of two soft boiled eggs, kippered herring or codfish, plenty of coffee with bread and butter and marmalade. At noon we dined off joints and potatoes with spotted dog pudding or custard. At four we had tea—big dishes of it with enormous slices of bread and butter and, twice a week, jam. Tea at this hour made it possible for me to go without supper.

My duties as time-keeper were easily managed.

Most of the men who did clerical work were elderly and settled, with little initiative, so that I found plenty of chance to help them. To do this I worked overtime, on Sundays and bank holidays, for which I received double pay.

Each pay day I turned over my whole wage to Mrs. White. Taking five shillings a week for room and laundry and giving me four shillings for spending money, she banked the rest for me.

As soon as my work had settled into routine I took part of my noon hour for making the rounds of the war offices. It was at the Red Cross that I learned there was such a thing in Paris as the Appleton Ambulance. An American Ambulance! With my experience as a driver of course they could use me! My hope soared.

From the Red Cross then I sought the London manager of the Ford company to learn the address of the Paris branch. After several attempts I was at last admitted to his office. A big fellow with legs like the pillars of the First Presbyterian Church back home, he sat dictating to his stenographer.

"What's your trouble?" he asked as uninvited I took a seat. He did not look at me. His efficient grey eye, hungry for more work, roamed the desk.

"I'm going to war," I said. "They won't have me here so I want to get a job in Paris till I can learn enough French to get into their army. I know Fords and I thought you might be so kind as to put me in touch through your Paris branch with the Appleton Ambulance."

"Sorry, young man, but I'm sure our Paris people can dispense with your services. Take my advice and go home. Now, Miss Witwer——"

"I beg your pardon." I rose. "Do you happen to know what mules are famous for?"

From the letter in his hand he looked up.

"I do," he said with emphasis.

"Exactly," I answered with equal emphasis. "And I didn't valet six hundred and thirty mules without catching it. I went through hell to get into this war and I'll get into it if I have to fight hell fires all the way to Paris. Good-day."

My hand was on the knob before he spoke. Then it was in a leisurely voice.

"Wait a moment."

I turned. His eye was still roaming the desk.

"What do you mean—valet six hundred and thirty mules?"

I told him.

"Sit down," he said crisply. He glanced over a letter. "The usual answer to this, Miss Witwer,

and you may go.   Now let's hear about the
mules."

Swinging his huge legs around from the desk
he gave a whole-minded attention to my story.
How surely he followed it I knew from the keen
questions that were the only break to my narra-
tive.   To my amazement I sat in this busy man's
office in London telling him about Sockeye and
Puggy, Pete and Sally, Marks' Yard and the bakery at home.

"You'll do, sonny," he said at last.   "I'll give
you a letter to a good friend of mine in Paris.
He'll put you where you want to go.   And if I
can do anything more for you let me know."

In highest spirits I almost ran back to work.   I
now had enough money to take me to Paris.   In a
few more days I should be in France!

My only problem was how to quit my job without playing a nasty trick on a company that expected its employés to grow grey in service.   Puz-
zling about it as I came down from tea that afternoon I heard a superintendent call to me, "Get
your hands out of your pockets, you, and move
along!"

I realised then that I had been indulging in
that ill-bred habit which, like spitting, is indige-

neous to America.⁵ But I realised, too, that here was my chance. I stuck my hands in deeper.

The superintendents, who swaggered about in frock coats, striped trousers and top hats, were treated by the men under them like Prussian royalty. This particular one was a ratty little man with a squeaky voice. Rushing at me now he caught me by the arm.

"Do you hear me?" he shrilled.

"Oh, speak up if you want to be heard," I answered, shaking him off. "Don't make a noise like a flea-bite."

He turned red, then purple. Never, it is safe to say, in his experience with those browbeaten British underlings, had he ever been insulted by an inferior. He tried several times to speak but spluttered and choked like a drowning man.

"Don't you fret," I went on insolently, "I'm going to clear out before you can sack me."

As soon as I could close up my work I hurried to the office of the staff superintendent. My sacking papers were before me.

"We're very sorry to lose you," said he, "but you must learn to be respectful."

"I didn't ask to stay," I answered. "I only want what's coming to me."

I was paid off immediately but hung around the

door till my little superintendent emerged onto the street. His face was still streaked with red, as if I had struck him. He was telling some one about my astounding impudence. I stepped in front of him.

"Next time you have anything to say to an American," I suggested, "talk to him as if he were a man or he may break your head."

A look of terror came into his face. I believe he thought I had lost my mind; not otherwise could he account for insubordination. I left him chattering as if he had a chill.

I was now free to go to France. At last, at last I was on the eve of Adventure!

With a sense of triumph I went next day to the American consulate.

"*You* still here?" demanded the important clerk who had advised me to go home. His tone showed surprise that I should have stayed in England against his will.

"Yes, I'm taking the next ship, as you suggested," I answered.

He looked gratified.

"Only it's bound for France," I added.

His face fell. Reluctantly he stamped my papers.

Now came two wearisome days at the French

consulate. From six in the morning till five at night I stood in line. But in the end I got my passport. By the time I had paid for it and for a third-class ticket to Paris I had only a few dollars left. But what did I care? Before the week was out I should be driving an ambulance to the front. Before the month was out I should be soaring above the clouds in my aeroplane. Yet, despite these high prospects, I said good-bye regretfully to the London bobby and his wife; they had proved to be the realest friends. I promised if I chanced to meet their son at the front to repay them. Then, bag in hand, I started by way of the American Express to the station.

The metropolitan calm of the mail clerk at the American Express had finally broken under my anxiety. Each day as soon as he caught sight of me he would shake his smooth head with a smile almost friendly. He had even a few days before written a personal letter for me to the Paris branch.

"I'm sure your mail's been held up there in some way," he said when I told him I had set the day for my departure, "and 'twill get here about two days before you leave."

Fretted by the probability that the letters had already come, those two days at the consulate had seemed endless. Now as I raced to the Express office all kinds of questions scampered through my mind. How was the business getting on without me? Would Jack write on coloured paper? How would she begin and end? Should I take time for a glimpse or should I wait to read luxuriously on the train?

"Produce 'em at once," I addressed the clerk whose back was towards me. "All prosecution will be dropped and no questions asked."

"Well, old man, they didn't come."

"Don't kid me, now——" I made a sick attempt to disbelieve him. "I'm in a rush. Cough up."

His look of sympathy quenched the flicker of hope.

"You're sure to find a batch in Paris," he said. "But if it crosses you on the way over, I'll send it right back. Good luck."

I wrung his hand and stumbled out. With one last look at the great awkward city sprawling over rain-soaked squares, I boarded the train for Dover.

I had waited too long, I had believed too often. I knew now that there would be no letters for me in Paris. Every one had deserted me—even my mother. As for Jasmine, she would not even trouble to tell me how completely I had dropped out of her life. I tried to fix my mind on the green folds of Sussex countryside silvered by the light English rain, the little spired villages that even in early spring possessed an air of leafy comfort; but my mind returned incessantly to its own bitter reflection.

Yet even through my disappointment Dover gave me a sudden glow. How often I had pictured it when as a boy I read Dickens's History of England! The adventurous, thick-nosed little ships with their sails puffing out in the wind that was to drive the warriors of Edward III to Calais —Calais that to the Englishmen of other times had always meant dazzling uncertainty; the tuniced archers who with bows cut from stout Engglish forest had pierced the armour of French knighthood at Poitiers—these merged in my mind with the modern little channel boat on which I now stepped.

There were English officers, English nurses— hardly any one else, in fact. And as I stood on deck looking back at the white cliffs which had once been a background for the adventurous, thick-nosed little boats loaded with archers and plumed knights, I heard an English voice drawling beside me, "There's nothing to it—I just jolly well climbed down into a funk-hole—that's all I was decorated for." It was a young English captain talking to a fellow officer. And as I heard the joking sureness of that voice, I realised that in a different slang but with the same spirit which must always make light of the duty it feels so keenly, the old archers had gone about their business.

Calais! What if I didn't know anything I had left behind? I was going to Calais! The French sea-town graven so deeply on the hearts of generations of Englishmen was once more insecure, this time from a different source. And I, the descendant of those old islanders who had crossed the channel, was crossing now to take my part, for England and for France.

When I stepped that night into the Gare du Nord exultation forsook me. The crowded station seemed like a prairie alive with grasshoppers. And as, with a forlorn hope of friendliness, I looked into each animated face, I could see nothing but the anxious vivacity of an insect bent upon filling its larder. So these were the French to whom I was offering my life! And this was France! For three months I had endured and denied that I might be here. And now that my feet were on French soil my heart—despised but still adoring—was under the magnolias.

In bitter mood next morning I went down to

breakfast at the cheap hotel near the station where I had spent the night. A bare-legged bandit mopping the floor paused long enough to bring me a tray, then returned to his bucket of dirty water. At the first taste of cold rolls and *café au lait* my American blood revolted.

"Slop under foot and slop under my belt," I commented aloud.

"*Oui, monsieur*," said the waiter.

He was a reckless-looking bandit and had he understood would doubtless have substituted me for the mop-rag. As he did not, it gave me a petty pleasure to murmur insults in the tone of polite nothings.

"Another bandit," I cooed to the maitre d'hotel when I went to pay my bill at the office. "Filth and son of filth, why aren't you in the trenches instead of robbing innocent travellers of their last buck?"

"*Oui monsieur*," he replied with a flash of teeth through his long black moustaches.

By the aid of a phrase-book I made him understand that I wanted to check my bag with him. Then, having found me fluently inclined, he asked when I had arrived in Paris. Feeling by now quite independent of the phrase-book I answered in my best French that I had come *demain*. He assured me, restrainedly at first, then wildly, that I was mistaken. I was firm. He gave me the lie. When the argument was growing heated I pulled out the phrase-book.

"Don't get excited, my friend," I reasoned with him as I went through the index, "or those little black beads you see through will fall off. They're loose now."

Then I looked up, crestfallen. *Hier* was the word for yesterday. I had been insisting that I came to-morrow. Upon my apologies he overlooked this extravagant claim and I set out into Paris.

It was an unkempt Paris that I saw, with narrow, reeking streets and ill-favoured houses and disordered traffic. Each driver pursued any course he chose; straight as a homing bird his instinct led him to some spot populous with drivers of identical taste. This harmony of purpose resulted invariably in a row.

"Pretty—bum—burg. El Paso, Texas, could knock the spots off its socks," I said. Then remembering my treatment at the hand of my native town, "But El Paso will never see *me* again. Not after the way my own mother has thrown me down."

With one more chance, however, I softened the

sentence for El Paso. I had two cards, one with the address of the American Express, the other with the address of the Ford Motor Company. In a café with the sign "English Spoken" I held up the first card. The girl at the cash desk pointed to a surface car. On the surface car, with a handful of change, I again held up the card. Taking out the proper fare the conductor let me off at the American Express.

"Byrd?"

I had sworn not to hope again. Yet my heart was following that bony hand.

"No mail for Byrd."

"You didn't forward it to London, did you?" My voice as I asked sounded hollow.

"No mail for Byrd," repeated the clerk impatiently.

"Thanks." My throat had gone dry. "If it comes, hold it."

"Wait!" At the mention of London a second clerk came up with a package. "Here's a special post from England for Byrd."

Whether the mistake was due to my sloppy handwriting or to the insecurity of wartime mails, I never knew. But the Paris office had never received my forwarding address. The letter from the London clerk was their first intimation of it.

And he had not failed me! The package must have reached London a few hours after my leaving.

Tearing open the bundle, I made sure of my mother's angular writing and another wayward hand. Then trying not to shout, I thrust the whole packet of letters and papers into my pockets and burst out the door.

What a different Paris from the one of five minutes ago—a Paris quivering with enchantment. I laughed with delight at the goats, which, herded along the pavement for their morning milking, looked about with wise, wicked faces. Every time a horny-cheeked driver bumped another horny-cheeked driver, I was charmed; when they stood up and shook their fists, each supported loyally by his inflammable freight, I felt that they were staging a French comedy for my special enjoyment.

I walked till I came to a little park. I opened a small white envelope, one of many like it. "Dearest Dicky," began the letter. I could read between lines all the sweetness she had shyly left unspoken. My heart was full. . . .

I heard the wavy song of a bird; the notes dipped and soared with winged flutterings. Trees were weaving over their bare arms a pale green lace. A robust young pine bowed to a maple which shook its golden curls in the breeze. . . .

Spring had come crashing down to earth. So it had come to me.

At the Ford Motor Company I found English-speaking people who took me at once to the Appleton Ambulance. There I put in my request to be sent to the front as a driver. During the three days required by the committee for passing upon my application I was to stay there at the hospital.

On the third day I was prepared to start. I was not prepared for the verdict.

"If you had come to us from New York that would have been different," said the committee-man. "But coming from England how do we know that you are an American?"

"You're right," I said after a stunned moment in which I could feel my face tighten with chagrin and disappointment, "with such limited intelligence as you people seem to possess I might be a Fiji queen for all *you* could tell. The Appleton Ambulance can go chase itself."

Fool, fool! I had written home that I was soon to be at the front. Now my one avenue was closed. Lee Malone would laugh at me, Jasmine would despise me. . . . I clenched my teeth. . . . I was not done for yet. For three months I had

drudged, half-starving, to find some way of fighting for countries that were spending thousands of
dollars recruiting men! Once more then I would
take up this ironical task.

First I tried another ambulance corps; my re-
jection by the Appleton unit was against me.
Next I filed an application with the French Aviation Corps and another for trench duty with the
Foreign Legion. I followed every cue, possible
or impossible.

While I waited for results I found a little café
where cabmen ate. Here I took one meal a day.
For twenty cents I could get bread with spinach
or string beans or soup. I used to look longingly
at the red wine; *I* was not a wealthy cabman.
Once or twice as a great luxury I treated myself to
roast beef. Another time I attempted to order
the good old American "ham an'." On the back
of the menu I drew an egg, then a strip of bacon.
The waitress was impressed by this display of
draughtsmanship, but seemed to think I was ex-
erting myself to amuse her. I drew another egg
and cackled. Then I drew another strip of bacon
and grunted. After a couple of cackles and grunts
I was rewarded by the coveted dish.

As my money dwindled I reduced my daily
meal to a big bowl of *café au lait* which I could

get with bread and butter for ten cents. Following my London plan I ate in the middle of the morning and went early to bed.

During this time I never lost a chance to pick up a word. My phrase-book, which contained such timely information as "Engines are made of iron," and "Do you like to be seasick?" was not of great service to a hungry man. I had to rely for sustenance upon such words as I could impale from the lips of waitresses and taxi-drivers. Once when I had pointed to a man's dish of soup the waitress called out, "*Chaud pour un!*" Pleased that I was mastering even French slang I went next day to another restaurant. "*Chaud pour un!*" I ordered. When the "warm for one" came it was not soup but coffee. This was sobering. If every café in Paris cited the language for its own purpose it would be long before I could use the vernacular.

However implacably I pursued that nimble tongue, I could not speak well enough to find work. Neither did I hear from any of my applications. I was growing so hungry that I spent hours in front of a certain bakery window feasting my imagination on the graceful outlines of bread and pastry.

So sure I had been of a driver's seat that I had

directed my mail to the Appleton Ambulance. And when time enough had passed for me to hear from home I went out to claim my letters.

Here was consolation! Starving I might be but the top letter of the pile handed out in response to my name was inscribed by the wayward hand I loved. Already light-headed with hunger the sight of it made me lunge a trifle unsteadily towards the desk.

"Know anything about an animal called the Ford?"

A twinkling voice addressed me. I looked up into a pair of green eyes that twinkled too.

"From snout to tail," I answered.

"Know anything about a man named Brown who herds the Fords in London?"

"Yes," I said in growing surprise.

"Did he ever mention a man named Foster?"

"Gave me a letter to him."

"You delivered it of course?"

"No——" My hand went involuntarily to my breast pocket.

"Why not?"

"Peeved at the Appleton Ambulance," I said somewhat sulkily.

"Well! I hope you're not too peeved to help me out. I'm looking for a chap that answers this description"—he pulled out a letter and began to mouse through it—" 'mules'—um, um—'tea and cake'—that's not it—'looks like a girl but has the guts of a gorilla'—here we are—'Face of a David on shoulders of Goliath. I'd have used him over here but he was headed for the front. He'll lick the gizzard out of some Boche.' How about it, Mr. Byrd?"

"I'm on, Mr. Foster," I said joyfully, forgiving even that disparaging comparison to a girl.

"Good!" He shook hands with me. His eyes which had twinkled respectively over my leaking boots and glossy trousers came back to mine. "If you had presented that letter," he said severely, "you'd have saved me the trouble of watching your mail and you wouldn't be looking like a Belgian orphan. Now I've got everything fixed and we're all to the mustard. So if you're not blasé after your debauched life of the past few months we'll see what you can do to a *filet mignon*."

No one save a man who had lived for three weeks on bread and coffee could appreciate to the full that jolly little celebration. With absolute impartiality I cleaned up everything from soup to cheese. Good food and good wine under my skin, the most delightful man I had ever met as host,

a job for to-morrow, Jasmine's letter in my pocket
—it was a night of heady satisfaction.

It was midnight when Mr. Foster left me at
my own door. At last I was alone with Jasmine.
Before tearing open the little white envelope I
touched it to my lips. . . .

Every drop of blood in my body rushed to my
heart. Was I going to faint? No, I must be a
man. With that resolution I put my head on the
pillow and cried like a woman.

After that it was a long time before I picked up
the letter to re-read it. Even then I made myself
do it. It was a kind of savage sentence of pain
upon myself. For now at last I knew that my
love for Jasmine was a weakness. Her spirit had
not touched mine, there under the magnolia. And
as with a knife-like pain I read each word over
again I saw Jasmine as she really was—cold and
soft and with oh, what a thrifty sense of keeping
what she seemed to refuse!

"We are far too young to think of such things
now, Dicky-bird." This was the paragraph that
stabbed me the most. "Perhaps after awhile when
you come back—but just now—well, how do you
know, perhaps you will meet somebody over
there."

She turned me down on the plea of my own in-

terest but I read beneath her generosity the calcu-
lation of it all. 'Twas she who did not want to
be fettered, she who was looking shrewdly into
the "perhaps" of these months while I was away.
In all this letter there was not one bit of tenderness. There was none of the mother heart in
Jasmine Gray.

There was no tenderness, no! What there was
in that heart was only a reckoning with the spectacular. Her vanity was asking to see herself in
the romantic rôle. When she had yielded to me
in the moonlit court she had yielded chiefly perhaps to the glamour of a departing soldier lover.
When she refused my offer now she refused a
poor vagrant, knocking shabbily on every back
door of the great war. If there were any tiny bit
of courage in my performance since I had left
her, she did not see it. She would see only the
trappings of courage. And when far down in her
letter I read the promise to come nurse me if I were
ever wounded, I saw in it only this grasping after
the spectacular situation.

Yet though I saw so plainly what I loved it did
not keep me from loving. I wanted her, I wanted
her! Let her come to me on any condition, only
let her come!

In my cheap little room under the kerosene lamp

on the oil-cloth covered table I began to try to justify her. Perhaps after all she *had* been thinking of me. Perhaps there was some little jealousy of the unknown in her letter. She may have been comparing me, who answered a call other than hers, with Lee Malone's faithless fidelity. Abjectly, hungrily, I searched her letter now with the determination to deceive myself.

CHAPTER III

THE Appleton Ambulance was just beginning to send out squads. Number One had gone to Dunkirk, Number Two to Pont-a-Mousson, Number Three to the Vosges. I had expected to be sent out with the fourth. I was detailed instead to look after the upkeep of cars for the field. This was a deep disappointment. An American office was a sterile spot for acquiring the native language. Yet French I must know before I could fight.

However I picked up what I could from the natives employed about the place. I was living in the hospital, an enormous building planned for a boys' high school but commandeered as it neared completion, for the Appleton Ambulance. In the unfinished attic we motor men had our dormitory. Our meals we took with the doctors and nurses.

With neither taste nor money for dissipation I could give every ounce of strength to my work. In a short time I was raised to the rank of assistant director with the relative rank of second lieutenant in the Ambulance Corps. Because of my first rebuff by the committee this slight honour gave me a gloomy satisfaction. It spurred me on, too, to greater effort. All day I worked tigerishly for the time when I could get into the fight.

During these weeks I never once heard from Jasmine. But the thought of her seldom left me. Always I hovered wretchedly between belief in her and the wish to keep her, whatever she was. The one thing I could not bear, the one possibility I would not even admit was of losing Jasmine. Better this torture than that the old feeling should go.

It was one morning in July and I was busy overhauling a car when Mr. Foster came up to me.

"Sonny," said he, "how'd you like to start to-morrow with a convoy of cars?"

"Start where?" I stared at him.

"To the front."

"I'd like it—fine," I said huskily.

*   *   *

I saw it, the mighty blue river of men flowing to the front. I was part of the sluggish stream that flowed after it. I heard the guns breaking upon the earth in wave on wave of thunder. I

was spattered with blood from the men I lifted
to my stretcher. Every torn body that rested in
my arms, every tortured eye that looked into
mine, bore a reproach. They seared me with
shame for my own empty purpose. However dear
Jasmine was to me she would never take care of
me now. I would fight, and die fighting, beside
those men.

*   *   *

I went back to Paris quivering and violent.

"A man's part is to fight—not to bring a fighter
home."

With rage in my voice I flung the words at
Foster.

"It's just a year," I went on, "since I began try-
ing to get into this war. And here I am, big and
young and husky, toting men who do the work.
Now I'm going to apply again to the Aviation
Corps and with a whole bunch to vouch for me
I ought to land this time."

I did land. The day was set for my examination.

I had counted on my knowledge of mechanics
to put me in the flying corps. But that was quite
superfluous. Indeed my whole examination was
a joke. While an American to-day, for instance,
is put through a dozen severe proofs of his sta-

bility as an aviator, mine was assured by the fact that I had once ridden a bicycle. The eye-test was equally facile. Even so, it almost shipwrecked me. I could read neither the letters nor the words on the chart and was forced to produce the spectacles I had carefully left outside. Even then I could not pass the test.

"No wonder, no wonder," said the specialist, taking the spectacles off my nose and squinting at them. "They are just plain glass. You need real spectacles, my boy."

He jotted down his report. So it was all up. It was bad enough to wear glasses at all. It was hopeless that I could not even see correctly through them. Despairingly I followed the reports to the office of the chief.

The chief read my name and age. When he came to my birthplace he paused. Was my nationality again to keep me out of the army as it had in England? My heart went down and down.

"Texas, U. S. A.," he read. "Is it then that you are a coo-boy?"

"I sure am," I said desperately. "Coyote County, Texas, and Sagebrush Sam is my middle name."

"Did you ever meet a gentleman"—he paused impressively—"called Buffalo William?"

"Knew him well when I was a child. He was a family friend. Used to ride me on his bucking broncho."

"And are you then familiar with the Texas steer?"

"She's just like a sister to me."

He gave a series of pleased little grunts.

I have since met many Frenchmen fascinated by the American frontier. Whether they have been influenced by Leatherstocking, or whether Cooper occupies the place he does on the French bookshelf because he strikes a responsive chord—I do not know. At any rate the chief, after a hurried shuffling of the reports on his desk, stood up and grasped my hand.

"You pass," he beamed.

With this useful past for an inducement, France had accepted me!

Next day I signed an engagement for the duration of the war with the Foreign Legion.

There were several hundred Americans already in various branches of the Legion. For this legion, awarded to France at the Hague Conference, gives any man the right to enter the French army and still retain his citizenship. He may have committed any crime, he may have received any sentence. But through the Foreign Legion he is born again. It is the international revival meeting, the great chance to start life clean. That it has lifted grizzliest sinners to heights seldom reached by the good man of lukewarm impulse— this is its appeal to the world's imagination.

As for me, I did not know how far I might go in it. I might never rise beyond mechanic. But I was part of the Foreign Legion. And my one regret now is that I never saw service with it.

For the present, however, I was thrillingly content. I had caught up with Adventure!

More exuberant than I had been for many weeks, I said good-bye to my friends at the Ambulance and started for Dijon. There I spent the night. Early next morning I walked four miles to the aviation department.

My arrival caused no ripple in that self-centred whirlpool. I tried to interest a harassed officer who only looked at me out of a haggard eye and went on. At first I was contented enough to watch the melodramatic characters that composed the Foreign Legion. A few approached the norm but most of them would have made Puggy and Sockeye look like preachers. In my worst nightmare I had never dreamed of such ruffians. For a few hours I followed these pirates about. But gradually their fascination paled. Noon passed. I was hungry and warm and tired. But not till evening did the harassed officer finally ask what I wanted.

"I want to know what to do," said I. "I'm an American."

He began then to hustle me around. Into one office after another he hustled me. After I had signed hundreds of papers, the import of which I was entirely innocent, he hustled me into the Bureau Habiliment and ordered for me the outfit of the French soldier. A weary clerk began tossing out clothes to me. The fit was a matter of luck. Seeing men grab shoes, I too began to accumulate footgear. My harvest consisted of one Number Seven shoe, one Number Nine, and two boots of incompatible temperament.

Then gathering up all my possessions I carried them outside for inspection. I found a coat and overcoat of horizon blue buttoning back from in front of the capot; trousers cut long to tie about the leg; puttees; two shirts of canvas ticking; one suit of underwear; two long strips of blue cloth, two rags and a long piece of red flannel. What the mission of these last three items I did not know. But they finally resolved themselves into cravats, handkerchiefs and a belly band. Fortunately I had socks and undershirts which here were considered needless luxuries. The rest of the outfit consisted of a knapsack, eating pan, cover, tin cup, knife and spoon.

I got into my uniform; the other things I attempted to pack. The knapsack however was so tiny that I could scarcely squeeze in the extra shirt. I sweat and swore till the combined perspiration and profanity moved an old soldier to show me how to fold everything in neatly.

I was then paid off at the rate of one cent a day for the three days I had belonged to the French army. Besides this sum total of three cents I was given a loaf of bread, a can of meat and a railroad ticket to the aviation school at Pau. Thus equipped I started the four mile walk back to town.

They were longer miles than I had walked in the cool of the morning. Six hours of standing about in the broiling sun had taken my zest. The knapsack fretted my unaccustomed shoulders. My boots did not fit. It was a subdued knight that presented himself at the hotel door.

I was pulling myself wearily up the steps to my room when I was astonished to see the landlady bar the way. Talking excitedly she would not hear my explanation. Then suddenly peering into my face she threw up her hands and laughed till she cried.

"*Mon pauvre, mon pauvre,*" she murmured, dragging me to my room.

I had left Dijon that morning in the trim khaki of the Appleton Ambulance. I had returned to Dijon in a costume that would have intimidated the bravest crow in the corn belt. My coat sleeves stopped just below the elbow. My trousers would have accommodated two of me. Used only to spirals, I had strapped these straight puttees on hind side before. No wonder the landlady did not recognise me. Yet I confess that her pitying enjoyment of my plight was my first experience in the horrors of war.

Next morning I left Dijon for Pau. As my route ran through Paris, I spent the night there. I wanted to call at the Ambulance but, trussed up as I was, would not expose myself to the rough blasts of friendship. So digging deep into my shallow savings I put up at a cheap hotel and by way of celebration that night invited myself to a liqueur at Maxim's.

So cloistered had been my life at the Ambulance that I was bewildered by the gaudy red place. Men and women pursuing pleasure with the anxious vivacity of the Parisian, *permissionnaires* packing their short leave full of gaiety—it was all as new as when I first came to Paris last spring.

A number of people, after the grateful fashion of the French with the soldiers, tried to be friendly. But as I was unable to answer and it never occurred to them that a man in horizon-blue could not speak French, they gave me up as a sour, surly fellow.

So in spite of its novelty Maxim's held little seduction for a penniless, badly-dressed, speechless stranger. Too lonely to enjoy it further I was about to pay for my liqueur and go to bed when a little girl, drifting by my table, threw me a smile. I smiled back, thankfully I suppose, for she sat down. I ordered coffee for the two of us. We were not able to say much to each other but making up in smiles we sat rather shyly sipping our coffee from the tall glasses. She was one of the blonde French with nose, eyebrows and mouth that tilted up. Long blue eyes, red lips, all her compact little figure surged with the sap of youth. My own youth responded. Less shyly now I leaned over to plant a long look in her eyes. I had forgotten that I was never again to be stirred by any woman. Her glance fluttered under mine and dropped to the gloves she was drawing through her hands. Then I noticed for the first time that the gloves were mine. How had she got them so quietly?

I had heard dark tales of cocottes. "She is going to implicate me in some way through those gloves," flashed through my mind.

Reaching over, I tried gently to take them from her but her fingers closed over them. I tried again less gently, but chattering like a magpie, she drew them back.

"Give me those gloves," I commanded.

"*Non, non, non,*" and she jerked them out of my hand.

As we had bridged our lingual difficulties before in smiles we now resorted to scowls and noise. Her face was red with anger and she kept up a constant stamping of her foot.

"You little devil———"

I didn't finish the sentence. She had slapped my face with the gloves. I got up so suddenly that I upset the table.

That was enough for the French public. With the same inflammable partisanship they brought to the support of their cabbies, they surrounded us. Some glared at me, some hissed at her, all buzzed like insects. In a second I was ushered out by a policeman. At the door a gendarme awaited me. I looked around desperately.

"Does any one here speak English?" I asked, raising my voice above the angry clacking.

Some one volunteered. I stated my case. He interpreted.

"Then we all go to court," decided the gendarme.

My suspicions of French courts were as dark as my forebodings about cocottes. I had heard enough rumour to know that my case was hopeless. They would never take my word against the girl's. I could not talk and she would be able to put up a fluent defence; this she was demonstrating now as she trotted beside the gendarme. I had disgraced my uniform. I would be thrown into prison. I could not report for duty at Pau. Probably I would be expelled from the army. And no one would believe that I had not stolen gloves from a poor cocotte! Sweat broke out on my face. Why, why had I gone to Maxim's?

Arriving at court I announced through the interpreter that the girl had stolen my gloves. My small opponent put up a vigorous counter accusation. I motioned to the sergeant to look at the stamp inside the gloves. It was that of an English firm. The little girl, not at all daunted by this evidence, said that this very afternoon an Englishman had given them to her.

To my absolute amazement the sergeant took my word, unhesitatingly, against hers. He ordered her to return the gloves. She refused. She stamped her foot and cried and stuck the gloves inside her blouse!

This would have routed American justice. Not so French. Two burly gendarmes seized her and after a scuffle in which one of them had his face scratched, they handed me the gloves. They were pretty rough with her so that I was sorry I had not let the gloves go and risked intrigue. But relieved inexpressibly at my own release I went back to Maxim's. And I could not resist, as I entered, giving the gloves an ostentatious flirt. Every one smiled.

In a moment my small enemy returned, red and ruffled, and still scolding.

"You little devil," I said, "you have your nerve to come back here."

With a toss of her head she stuck out her little red tongue. At this the smiles of the crowd broke into laughter in which I joined. Then, having established my honesty, I went back to my room. As I took off my overcoat my own gloves, made by the same well-known firm, fell out!

"Oh, damn!" I said aloud.

I knew that I had been a cad. I knew that I should go back to find my little victim. But as I could not make myself understood I should probably be arrested. And I had worked too hard and too long for my uniform to have it taken from me now.

"Damn, damn, damn," I kept repeating in bed as I thought of the way the gendarmes had handled her. I often wondered afterwards what that poor little *poule* thought of the American that stole her gloves; and the wonder always brought a blush.

* * *

I spent the next night at a hotel in Pau which, by the way, ate up my next year's pay. Next morning I walked from the town to the aviation camp. As I drew close I began to run. When I could see the big muddy field with its long rows of portable buildings, its immense canvas hangars and skylights, its great winged planes rising and falling, when I recognised the place where Wilbur Wright had given exhibitions—then I broke into wild whoops. I was here, I was here!

In the *Barrack des Etrangers* where I was sent I found natives of every nation in the world—unless it was Germany. I found Mexicans, Cubans,

Russians, Peruvians, and men from countries that I did not know existed.

The matted sound of all these strange tongues wrapped me in isolation. If there were just one choice spirit to savour with me this hour! Defeat I could bear unsupported but triumph—what was triumph without some one to share it? Even at this supreme moment when I stood at the gate of Adventure I was conscious that I stood alone.

But the great fact was that I was here. I hurried out. I could not keep my eyes off the air through which big and little craft moved with wings steady or uncertain.

"Take her easy now, youngster. You'll feel better soon. To-morrow yuh can sit up awhile and the next day yuh can have a little gruel."

The nasal intonation, the sloppy speech, the jeering of my native land! Leaving the sky my hypnotised gaze lighted on two lanky forms both in horizon-blue and both unmistakably American. Hull I had met at the Ambulance. Payne I knew by reputation for his service in the trenches. As I gripped their hands I felt my mouth widen in a grin of joy. I still stood at the gate of Adventure. I no longer stood alone.

*   *   *

I was ready to leave El Paso. The whole town was out to see me off. "What a pity the census-taker isn't here," thought I, "it would save him weeks of work." The mayor was making a speech. My mother was smiling. The fellows were clamouring for a last shake of my hand—all except Lee Malone who skulked by himself. The girls were cheering. Jasmine—Jasmine was begging me to kiss her—before all those people! I was torn between embarrassment and pride on the one side, on the other my deep desire. Night fell magically and curtained us with dark solitude. I sought for her soft lips, sought and found them. My pulses beat tumultuously. I had meant to be only kind. I had not meant to be drawn down, down, down, deeper and deeper into the deadly sweetness of those lips. I fought against them. "Take me with you." She drew her slender hands down my face. "Take me with you." She held up her arms and leaned against me. My senses swam. We two alone in the clouds. Her lips would be mine in a world-long kiss— *but how could I fly?* She must not come *during*, she must come *after*. Attainment first, then the sweet reward. "When I come back," I whispered, "then I will take you." I jumped into the car and shouted "Contact!" The ropes were cut. Up I soared and off, over prairies and mountains and cheering cities and oceans. Far below, far behind trailed Jasmine and my world of home. They would reach Germany just in time to see me face a winged army, face it, conquer it——

"We can't get 'em up, we can't get 'em up,
   We can't get 'em up in the morning!"

How strange to hear the old American réveillez here in Germany!

"Hell!" I shouted angrily. "Who's making this row? I was right on the Crown Prince's tail, too!"

"Five-thirty," said Payne from the bunk next mine. "Jump up and jump in, you poor simp."

Hustling out of bed he dipped his tin cup in a bucket of black coffee that a man was carrying through the barrack.

With an unnatural politeness due to a brain still too dazed by dreams of love and world-power to fight off the hungry mob, I didn't get my share. But it was the last time that courtesy interfered with my brimming mug of hot coffee; for it was our only nourishment until noon.

Following the example of Hull and Payne I jumped into my clothes and hurried out to the field where we were due at a quarter to six. After

reporting there we came back to barracks to roll
our mattresses and sleeping sacks. Next came
Appeal when the daily report of punishments and
duties was read. A bunch of men was fined—
some for going to Pau without permission, some
for not wearing their coats to town, some for being
late at Call.

Practice lasted from ten-thirty till noon. Then
after a meal of beef with beans, macaroni or potatoes we could rest till two. Second practice began
then and lasted till it was dark.

Although I was not yet posted for duty I could
not stay off the field. Around and around I
walked, just inside the fence out of the way of machines.

It was not yet seven o'clock of my first day. I
was watching a flier some thousand feet up. Suddenly he dove. He pulled up his machine but it
hit the ground. The tail, breaking in two, dug a
hole a foot deep. I was the first to reach the poor
chap. I helped carry out the body. For an hour I
trembled like a girl.

And yet the field drew me. My eyes scarcely
left the sky. That very day I was watching two
machines. They drew close to each other—dan-
gerously close, it seemed to me . . . I cried out.
They bumped in midair. They dropped, they

struck. Once more I was the first to reach the machines. Once more I helped carry out the dead. In less than twelve hours I had seen three men killed. I leaned up against the wall and was sick. And still the field drew me. I stayed away from it only to snatch food and sleep.

In spite of my gruesome initiation my own desire was mounting. When could *I* begin? On the third day came my answer. I was given my number. Fifty-six! This meant that fifty-five others would be called before I could even start training.

With other pilot students then I was put on field duty as mechanic. All day we turned the tails of other men's machines.

A month passed. I was still turning tails. Should I never fly? Should I spend the rest of my life in one treadmill after another? Was I who burned to roam the skies to be a "penguin" rolling on the ground?

But the penguin does give place to fleeter craft and turning tails did come to an end.

On a white, misty morning in October I began practice.

Trundling back and forth over the muddy field in my short-winged Bleriot was absorbing enough for a day or two. Then I wanted something crag-

gier for my energies. But I had to content myself with perfecting my technique.

There was no dual control in this school. The
pilot was required to learn every step by himself.
So I had to learn the movements in three different
penguins before I was promoted to a machine with
full-sized wings. In this I could leave the ground
by one or two feet, making the thousand yards to
the end of the field in a series of jumps. Then
with the motor sped up I rose a yard or two and
made a little landing.

In my next machine, of the same type but higher
power, I dove a bit and corrected my motions so
as to make a smoother landing. It was like taking
a dancing lesson in the air—circle to the left, turn
to the right, back to the centre, turn to the left. I
learned to keep the machine in perfect poise. By
tipping the wings I learned to make a precarious
bow. I did figure eights. I glided, turning at the
same time I glided.

One hundred yards, two hundred yards, five
hundred yards! Hour by hour, day by day, foot
by foot, yard by yard, I was gaining on Adventure. If I could have stepped into the car and
flown off, that would have been conquest. But so
gradual was the ascent that I could hardly feel
myself mounting. Even the official spiral was

just another scramble up the slopes. Not till I could take my cross-country flight would the peaks be mine!

The weather all that autumn was windy or rainy or foggy or lowering. Any of these conditions was bad for cross-country flying. I had always thought that my will could dominate any situation but I had always thought of the will to act. Now I had to acquire the will to wait.

In such torpor Jasmine's image, submerged in more tumultuous hours, would rise up to torment me. Sometimes at night in spite of my longing, perhaps because of it, I would decide with finality not to forgive her. At last I knew that I had finished with her, irrevocably. In this bitter peace the sleep that crept over my exhausted body would flow up into my brain until it caught and drowned each fleeting thought . . . sleep deep and dreamless as the sea . . . then disturbed memories that hovered over the depth . . . memories that plunged and brought me up out of the brief, kind stupor into living pain. My eyes would be wet; I had cried in my sleep. Evoked by dreams, the image would linger among my waking senses . . . the dark Spanish eyes with their tropical warmth that was not warmth, the fruity hair and cheeks, the little fragile fingers. I could hear the rustling voice. I could see her as she looked up at me the first time we had danced together. I could feel the freshness of her lips in the perfumed darkness under the magnolias. And in that hour of lonely yearning before dawn I would murmur the words I had written her: "I never cared for any one but you. I never can. I'm not going to give up yet. But don't forget one thing—that when I'm wounded you're to come over and take care of me."

After such a night as this my only relief was to walk. Feverishly I took long, exhausting hikes until my throbbing muscles promised oblivion at night. During these days I had one companion. Hull and Payne had already completed their courses and gone on. And, as my accomplishments did not include a familiarity with Russian, Peruvian or Chinese, I had to confine social intercourse to an English-speaking Jap.

The Jap was a gallant fellow. He could fly fairly well but he could not land. "What do you do when you want to land?" I asked once, curious about the mental make-up that, with his will and intelligence, inhibited this one feat. "I cut my motor, I dive, I close my eyes, I wait." This was what he literally did. And every time he tried to land he smashed a machine. With Oriental toughness he persisted. But he cost the government so much in machinery that the captain decided to discharge him. It is of course such a disgrace for a Jap to start anything he can't finish that Moiche threatened hari-kari. And to prevent the spectacle of a disembowelled student, the horrified captain let him stay. After I left I received one letter from him. It began: "Dear My Friend Mr. Richard Byrd." I learned soon afterwards that, still attempting the landing he was never able to make, he had been smashed to the ground near his hangar.

While I was still at Pau we spent many hours together walking through the fiery autumn woods. Next to landing his ambition was to master American slang. In return for what I taught him he gave me a few lessons in Japanese. And it was in the midst of one of these strange studies that an officer summoned me. To-morrow had been set for my cross-country flight!

The sheltered quiet sunshine that had made Pau famous as a winter resort had come at last. Fog and wind had gone. It was a still December morning when Moiche helped me into my fur combination. I was to fly fifty miles south over a small town, return without landing and fly fifty miles west. Then would follow the official triangle and my training was complete.

My flesh, which had tingled deliciously with the cold when I first stepped out on the field, was now creeping with another sensation. As, calmly pulling down my helmet and up my gauntlets, I walked to the machine, I trusted that no one would notice how the calves of my legs wobbled. Fastening my safety belt, I settled myself fussily.

"Contact!" called the mechanician.

"Cuh-cuh-contact!" I chattered.

"Cuh-cuh-cold feet!" jeered Moiche, tempted from his usual eastern courtesy by this chance to display his learning.

Some one laughed. There seemed an extraordinarily large number of visitors.

Taxi-ing across the field I came back, mounting in circles. I had expected a kind of trance in which mundane things would disappear. But there were the narrow eyes and fat little mouth of Moiche, the stiff black head of the mechanician, the square upturned face of some visitor, his arms thrust into his overcoat pockets. How disappointing——

Just then my motor took the bit in its teeth and galloped off. "Whoa, whoa!" I shrieked, then was glad no one could hear me. My hands felt suddenly small and weak. How could *I* quiet this roaring, snorting monster of energy tearing over space? I clutched the controls. The movement grew smoother and stiller. From the tail of my eye I cast down a furtive glance. The earth was backing away. The old castle, the moat and drawbridge, the canal, the twisted rope of water—all were backing off from me as fast as they could go. Even the pine forest was floating away like a green veil blown from a woman's shoulder. I threw an elated thought to Jasmine and to mother. I had caught up with Adventure!

I was one with the eagle. I sat between its potent wings. I was fleeter than the wind. I was lighter than those luminous clouds below me. I awakened the dawn. I opened the gates of the morning. I tread the rays of the sun to the sun's rim, and it quailed before me.

In a fairly decent landing I slid down to earth.

"Oh boy, oh boy," was all I could say as picking Moiche up by the shoulder-blades I fox-trotted him across the barracks.

*   *   *

Then came the official triangle. On it I flew south to a small town, made a landing, flew west for another landing and then flew back to the field. This was not accomplished so quickly as it might have been. For of course like every other aviator I was lost on my triangle and landed near a quaint,

red-roofed village, where the mayor and the
schoolmaster grew heated over the honour of en-
tertaining me.

I explained to the city fathers that since the
schoolmaster spoke English I would spend the
night with him. Probably no one suspected that
this decision was influenced by the dominie's pretty
daughter. It was a happy choice. The supper of
onion soup, omelette soufflé and wine served me by
Madame before the ruddy hearth, the eager questions of Monsieur about the craft and art of flying,
the ripe black eyes and ripe red lips of Mademoiselle—these made me glad I had forsworn the
mayor's more imposing entertainment for the hos-
pitality of this little stone cottage.

This official triangle gave more leisure than the
cross-country flight for the enjoyment of my own
sensations. They had lost no exultancy. I had
discovered a new world. Its foundation was a sea
of clouds. It was established on sunlit floods.

The last test was one of height. After staying
up an hour at an altitude of two thousand yards I
received my brevet. I was now a pilot and ordered
to a second school at Laon.

Christmas I was invited to spend at the Appleton Ambulance. So with my wings and star and
corporal's stripe to take the curse off my shoddy

uniform I reached the Gare. du Nord in holiday fettle.

Paris too was in festal mood. The air was cold and brilliant and tonic. The city was distilling its perfume—the tantalising smell of baking bread, frying onions, roasting chestnuts; sweat of horses; motors exuding gasoline; scented garments of women; spicy breath of carnations in the florist's window; pungent whiffs of bay-rum through the barber's door. The city was making its music too —the clash of wheels against the cobble-stones, the tangled skein of voices and the faint, far sound of the guns. The black stream that flowed down the boulevards was touched with currents of horizon-blue and ruffled with gleams of feminine brightness. As I made my way to the Ambulance, every sense carolled its enjoyment of the sights and sounds and smells of Paris.

Thanks to the wings on my collar I found myself a bit of a hero. There was at the Ambulance a tendency to fête me, one which, because of my shaggy appearance, I started to protest.

But the "Foster-Father" of the Ambulance as my first and best friend there was called, had anticipated my vanity. Foster himself, beyond the age for more active service, did his part in a dozen other ways. One of them was the treats he was always giving the boys. Dinners, gifts, money smuggled into one's possession—by such means did Foster make life more livable for young Americans in the war not yet their own. Perhaps because my determined efforts to get into service had amused him, he was even more of a foster-father to me. So now, aided by the measurement of my khaki, he had ready for me a finely tailored uniform, worthy the wings that were at once transferred to it. In the pocket he had left a thick roll of greenbacks. "Christmas Evergreens," they were labelled.

"That's enough," he said when I tried to thank him. "King and Stoner left word there was to be a meeting of all American aviators at Louey's Café at five to-day. I'm giving you a chow-party to-night. And I want you to be a credit to the A. A."

There were other gifts, too—candy and cakes from Mother, cigarettes from the boys, and from Jasmine—yes, from Jasmine—a small, flat parcel. With quickened breath I wrenched off the wrapper. Herself! The great eyes looked softly into mine, the full curved lips repeated their old magic. My heart gave a throb of pain. It was her first message since that fateful letter. As always, she had known the best way to keep my heart aching.

I tucked the little photograph into the pocket of my new uniform. It lay there beside the stiff, green bills. For a moment I stood helpless under the rush of that old feeling. Then with a bitter recovery I started for the door. Jasmine was not all. I was twenty-one. I was wearing the aviator's uniform. It was Christmas Eve. As I strode through the long halls of the hospital I was repeating these things to myself. For the first time I faced what is so difficult for youth to face—the fleetness of grief, the powers of the future.

It was just as I reached the doorway of the last ward that I saw a nurse reaching up to straighten a festoon. Squarely under the mistletoe! I was reckless with my new, hard optimism. Clasping an arm about the whiteclad figure I was about to go further. Her back stiffened as she whirled about and Irish eyes faced me stormily. I fell back. I recognised those eyes at once. It was the girl I had seen wheeling the crippled soldier in the Dublin station, the girl who had picked me out for her merry, tonic smile of inquiry.

"Beg pardon—Cussmas—American kisstom," I stammered into the outraged face. "I'm awfully sorry—truly."

"Oh—it's *you*, is it? You'd better be sorry!"

She remembered me! I tingled with triumph.

Even in the change from my mongrel livery of that Dublin night to this natty horizon-blue, she remembered!

"What are you doing in that uniform?" I asked at last. Then realising my inanity I blushed.

"Oh," said she casually, answering the blush, "shoeing horses, digging potatoes, cutting lumber —all the little things expected of a nurse in the hospital. What are you doing in *that* uniform?"

"Oh," answered I, "mending the baby's clothes, putting up preserves, arranging the flowers—all the little things expected of a flier on the field."

We both laughed. Then with a little nod she started off.

"*Don't* go," I begged in dismay. "I haven't seen a woman for months." I would have caught at her hand but was too thoroughly intimidated.

"None of them have, poor dears," she answered pityingly.

She put her head on one side and looked at me as if she were denying a child.

"And I'm running away from my boys to-night so I mustn't neglect them now."

I looked after her. Why, I wondered ungratefully, didn't that donkey of a Foster ask *her* to-night? By jove, I would make him do it yet. As I turned back to find him I remembered that I didn't know her name. But I would describe her. Little—oh, very little, blue eyes, dash of brogue, black curly hair, crisp walk. I stopped short. She had said she was going out to-night.

"Oh, damn," I muttered. "Well, I'll look her up to-morrow."

I was the last to arrive at Louey's Café, where there was a jovial reunion between Hull, Payne and myself. There were three older men, too, already distinguished fliers, whom I had never met. As I looked over the crowd I remembered some one's definition of an aviator—a womanly warrior. The two airmen most renowned were especially true to type. King's square chin and enduring eyes were those of a soldier but his dimples and delicate brows would have lent charm to a girl. Stoner, long-limbed, high-bred, was sensitive as a poet, unswerving as an explorer.

Warm-blooded and hardy from camp life, we chose a pavement table in the cold, medicinal sunshine. All of us, I think, were in a pleasant commotion. We sniffed something epic in the air. But not till our glasses were filled, not till his cigar glowed steadily, did King relieve our impatience. A man of wordless force he made what was for him a long and eloquent speech:

"Fellows, there are now half a dozen of us

breveted pilots from the U. S. A. Why don't we
get together and form an American Squad?"

Puffing his cigar excitedly, he looked into one
face after another. We were quiet at first under
what seemed to us an epoch-making suggestion.
Then the spark slowly caught. We took fire. We
pounded the table, we clashed our glasses.

It was some time before King could bring us
down to earth. There were many details that must
be taken up with many officials. These we had to
work out now; in a few days we should all be
scattered. So abandoning future romance we
buckled down to business.

When he had made our arrangements we shook
hands.

"The next time we six meet together, it will be
as the American Squad," said Stoner, and at this
we shook hands again. Then as we scattered I felt
a sudden hollow in my stomach. Eight-thirty—
Foster's dinner was at eight! I had forgotten it
completely. Half an hour late, I jumped into a
taxi.

I was bumped out at Margery's by a head-on
collision with another taxi. As I scrambled out
the two chauffeurs opened fire.

"Treat 'em rough," I shouted, tossing a coin

to my driver and wishing I could stay to get my money's worth.

As the door of the enemy car gave way out burst a small woman in a gold-embroidered evening wrap. Expecting her to cudgel me over the head I was about to flee when a hand clutched my arm. I looked down in trepidation.

"Oh," said the voice with the dash of brogue. "I'm glad you're late too. Mr. Foster will be so cross. I just couldn't leave my boys earlier on Christmas Eve!"

Her red upper lip caught at a smile that was trying to run off and hide. I thought her inconsequential acceptance of me delightfully feminine.

"We'll rig up a reason," said I as with my hand under her elbow we hurried in. "You receive urgent letter from unknown woman imploring you to save her at eight o'clock sharp to-night. You doll up for dinner and drop around on the way. Entering dark hovel, find Slippery Sal the Sandbag Siren. Aided by Roughneck Nolly she is about to relieve you of life and jewels when I, Peter Punchbag, disguised as chauffeur, rush in, fire one thrifty shot for the two of 'em—and here we are alive but hungry!"

"It's easy to guess what high-grade literature *you* hid under your geography—oh, here comes

Mr. Foster. How distinguished he looks in evening dress!"

He was a striking figure with his tawny, leonine head towering over the crowd and his tawny, twinkling eyes, that just now looked somewhat severe.

"So you two have met already," said he, piloting us to a table in the corner where sat a hilarious group of girls in dainty frocks and ambulance men in khaki. "We just this minute sat down— thought we wouldn't wait more than half an hour for the guest of honour."

That started me on an apology.

"Hist!" interrupted my companion. "Don't forget Peter the Punchbag and Soapsuds Sal!"

At that Foster relaxed and with a laugh placed her at his right.

"Foot of the class for you, young man," he said to me.

I wished I could have sat beside her. I had so much to say to her. So, evidently, had Foster. Her head was half the time turned to him. Then I could see only her white neck from which the hair waved upwards black as midnight. Sometimes when Foster, turning to the little blonde on his left, relinquished her for a minute, she would look around at me. Then I discovered that everything about her was full of nooks and crannies. A smile would break up her face into new little niches. Her voice, a sparkling, sunny voice, kept dropping into strange depths and coming up in some unexpected bright spot. The laughter in her eyes was always going down behind shadows, then rising to brush them aside. Once when Foster pledged *"The Buzzard,"*—the old nickname of which I had told him always amused him—"and his new pair of wings," her eyes were on me in some unsmiling thought that chilled me. What was she thinking about? Then as the laughter broke from behind the shadows I was suddenly warmed again.

It was a night of triumphant happiness. After months in a muddy barrack how contenting was all this elegance—gleam of silver and linen and white shoulders, brightness of holly, delicious food and champagne. Nor was I insensible to my own small notoriety, especially in the light of those eyes with the nooks and crannies.

Next morning I was the first one down. I was determined not to miss her. It was not long before I saw the crisp little figure in its crisp white uniform.

"Good morning Merry Christmas will you dine with me to-night?" I asked in one unpunctuated breath.

"Good morning Merry Christmas no I won't," she said. Then seeing my face she added, "You see my boys have been talking for days about the Christmas tree I'm going to give them to-night. I really couldn't leave, could I?"

"But that will be over early," I insisted. "We'll make it nine o'clock."

"Two nights running? That's dissipation." She shook her head. "I really mustn't." Her face brightened. "But I guess I will."

"Hurrah!" I said. "I'll call for you."

I spent the rest of the day picking out a secluded table in an unsecluded café, composing a menu, studying wines, procuring poinsettias. If it took my last penny I was determined to have a perfect setting.

"Foster's Christmas greenery was a life-saver this time," I thought fereventitly.

Her pleasure when she saw the poinsettias was more than reward for the miles I had trudged to find them.

"For a young man whose earning capacity is just a cent a day, aren't you a bit extravagant?" she asked, surveying the table with delighted disapproval.

"A few months on the field makes a fellow feel

as if he'd earned a Christmas tree," I answered
with a joyous grin.

"You have, indeed, poor darlings," she said
with one of those sudden cloudings in her eyes.
"Do you know, here I sit eating dinner with you
—and such a dinner—without knowing your
name?"

"I don't know yours either," I beamed. The
situation, as well as those echoing eyes, conjured
romance. "Let's see how long we can keep 'em
dark and have private names for each other."

"That's easy. I tagged you the first time I
saw you."

As I looked up inquiringly a verdant note
struck my sight. It was a green frock in the doorway. Above it shone the long blue eyes and yellow hair of my little *poule*.

"Oh, pardon—wait a minute!" I interrupted.
"I must speak to that girl.

Getting up so suddenly that I spilled the wine,
I made my way to the door. In my new uniform
she did not recognise me but, as I bade, followed
me to the dressing-room. There I produced the
gloves her Englishman had given her. I knew
enough French now to present a humble apology
and with it one of Foster's greenbacks.

At sight of the gloves she remembered. At

sight of the money she forgave. Gibbering like
a monkey she caught my hand and, to my utter
horror, kissed it. She even pressed upon me her
name and address.

"If you ever need a friend," she said. Indeed
I had some trouble in getting rid of her.

When I sat down again, the soup was steaming,
the glasses were filled. Still brilliant were the
flowers, the silver, the napery. Only my companion had changed. Gone was the merry, tonic
smile. She was looking after the girl I had just
left with a speculation almost wistful. Yet there
was nothing of petty, personal vigilance in the
glance she gave to this poor moth of the street,
none of the feminine anger which Jasmine would
have felt. It was a look so big with thought of
others, so filled with a sense of danger which she
could not avert—she was thinking so pitifully of
the girl, so sadly of me . . . Before this widened
spirit of hers my eyes fell. And afterwards as
I told her the little story I kept thinking to myself, "And she's pretty, too!"

CHAPTER IV

AFTER that moment even my lightest banter was tinged with this sudden sharp reverence.

"Just how young are you?" she asked as I finished my story and the smile which, always trying to escape to some nook, was caught and brought back severely by her mouth.

"My public age is twenty-two. I lied to get my passport. Just how young are you?"

"Twenty-three is my public age. I lied to get *my* passport."

"You look about eighteen and act about thirty," I volunteered.

"It's *not* a pretty thing to say to a woman," I heard her say.

"I mean," I floundered, glancing up to see if she were serious, "that you seem like a born mother."

A mysterious little smile, not at all motherly, came into her eyes. I grew embarrassed.

118

"You didn't tell me your name for me," I said rapidly.

"The Swallow," she answered. Seeing my look of uneasy inquiry she added, "Oh, it's all right. You looked so downy and unfledged and eager, with your soaring eyes. Just poised for high flights somewhere."

"Downy?" I gave a scowl reminiscent of the dicky bird.

"Ruffled, now, if you prefer that," she appeased me. "And what are you going to call me?"

"Let me think—you reminded me of the sea."

"The sea! Gullish—fishy—full of craft—or what?"

"No," I said emphatically, eyeing my plate, "Salty, bracing and deep. You made me feel as if you'd been to unknown places, like the sea, and no man could know where you'd go next. Smooth and sunny, but full of storm. I like the sea. I like anything invigorating." I said this breathlessly, not daring to look up. Then as it drew no response I drove it home. I raised my eyes with a boldness I did not feel. "I like you, too," I added.

She, too, was gazing steadily at her plate.

"Why?" she asked.

"Because you know men and say the right

thing and are always just around the corner. In other words, because you're a real woman." Then I became heady with happiness. "Why do you like me?"

"Because," she answered gravely, "you don't know anything about women and say the wrong thing and are always this side the corner. In other words, because you're a real man. Well, Swallow, what are you going to call me?"

"The Stormy Petrel is the best I can think of."

"Your description sounded more like an old salt. But now tell me about *her*."

"*Her!*"

"I *must* have this to play with. It's so satiny." She put out a ruthless white hand and tore off a poinsettia petal. Then her calm gaze returned to me. "Yes, the girl at home—the one you brought me here to talk about. You may have thought you brought me for other reasons but you didn't."

Knowing this to be the truth I ate my chicken in stubborn silence.

"Begin farther back," she commanded in tactful impatience, tapping the stem of her glass with a gleaming pink nail. "I must know from the beginning. What is your mother like?"

My mother! I walked straight into the trap.

"My mother is the bravest soldier I ever knew."

Those words broke down my feeble reserve. As she had ordered I began at the beginning. Like a dumb man suddenly restored to speech I talked on and on. When I had brought my biography up to date, when I had told her of the letter that had blighted and broken me—then I pulled out the little photograph.

"How awfully pretty!" she exclaimed, bending over it. "How awfully pretty!"

"She sure is," I agreed, proud of her praise. "It was tough to be turned down by a girl like that, but I haven't given up."

"Turned down!" She erected two small thumbs. "You are no more turned down than these are. Take my word for it."

"Do you mean she'll marry me?"

My companion found a sudden interest in her pastry. Then she asked quietly, "When did you expect to marry?"

"Why, when I get through seeing life."

"Ah, now you have answered your own question," was her cryptic answer. "But will you *please* look at the time? Take me home as fast as you can. I think you're more of a bat than a swallow."

"I can't seem to get out of the feathered kingdom," said I, helping her into her cloak. "Started life as a dicky bird, was promoted to a buzzard, metâmorphosed into a swallow——"

"And now go owling about Paris corrupting the habits of a respectable petrel."

At her door I leaned my shoulders against the wall, prepared for an hour of pleasant farewell. This plan was rudely upset by a small hand thrust out at me. There was finality in its grasp.

"Thank you so much, Swallow. You're going to write to me," she announced calmly.

"I sure am," I agreed.

"And I shan't answer."

"Oh, you must!" I begged. "I'll be so lonely."

"All of them are, poor dears." She put her head on one side and looked at me again as if she were denying a child. "And I can't write to all of them."

"I'm not one of *them*," I protested. But she was gone.

When I got to my own room in Foster's quarters I jerked out my fountain pen and began to write.

"My dearest one——" I was beginning a letter to Jasmine. Usually when I wrote to her I had to fight my pen to hold it back. Now to my amazement I could not think of a word to say.

"Your picture came on Christmas Eve——"
Finally I accomplished this much. Well, well,
what then? I commenced making little geo-
metrical figures around the edges of my paper. At
last I took her picture from my pocket and set it
up on the table in front of me. I looked at it
studiously, conscientiously . . . "You looked so
downy and unfledged and eager" . . . Merry
blue eyes came between me and the picture and
I was smiling imbecilely in reply. The smile
died down as another look interposed between me
and the picture—a look so filled with sadness over
dangers not her own, a look so wistfully protect-
ing that I thrilled again with the memory.

Suddenly then I jumped to my feet. In bewilderment that was almost grotesque I stared at
myself in the mirror.

"Well, of all——" I said, dumfounded.

     *   *   *

Laon was near enough the Alps for us to taste
the mountain cold. The camp was new. We
walked to our knees in mud. Water stood deep
under the barracks. As we had no stoves and
only one blanket, we slept in our overcoats.

Since there were not enough chassé machines
to go around I was assigned to a voisin. After
flying a monoplane, the big, unwieldy biplane

seemed an indignity. I had, too, to fly the Caproni, an immense Italian machine with three motors of one hundred and fifty horse-power, capable of carrying five men.

  The type of machine we used at this time had the habit of catching fire. Quite a number of the fellows were burned. Every time one of our men met this most horrible of all deaths, the whole school attended the funeral. It became a weekly experience—that horrified, blackened thing leaping from the falling monster of fire; the procession of bluecoated comrades; the bare-headed villagers, crossing themselves; the service in the old cathedral, heavy with incense, misty with the light of tapers.

  Although I did not have to follow the line of training prescribed at Pau I put in many hours of drudgery before my apprenticeship was considered sufficient; for it was drudgery to fly those heavy bombarding machines. But when I could reach a height of fourteen hundred yards and up, there I found reward. They would fall farther and farther away—the buttressed hill above the little plain, steep vineyards, turreted palace and Gothic cloister and the old cathedral towered like a fortress—until they were nothing but a doll's establishment. Then like one blunt spear-end in a row of dagger points, Mont Blanc would rise among her clustering peaks. I could see a blue patch that was Lake Geneva. I could see the whole valley of the Rhone—a gossamer veil threaded by one silver cord that frayed out into tiny strands of silver. Again I had reached the sun-sluiced peaks of Romance!

During these busy days I had thought incessantly of my next visit to Paris. I wanted to tell that girl at the Ambulance everything that had happened since I saw her. I liked to remember the clever things I had said and to construct more scintillating dialogue. With that trip in view I was cultivating a moustache. This ornament was so white at first that the boys named it Mont Blanc. "Maybe it will turn red or some other pretty colour," they encouraged me. Darkening with age and weather it finally became a rusty black like old mourning. I was more than pleased with it. And just in time it turned. For I was transferred to the military field that protects Paris from night raids. Now I should see her often!

I reached Paris early in the morning. Bathed, polished, with Mont Blanc neatly trimmed, I presented myself at the Ambulance.

The first person I saw was herself. She was bending over some charts on her office desk.

"Good morning," I said optimistically; "you're dining with me to-night."

The springy little white figure straightened.

"Oh! How do you do? I *wish* I could."

She gave me her left hand and a hurried smile while with her right hand she jotted down something on a slip of paper. She did not even notice Mont Blanc. I was alarmed. Then I remembered her weakness.

"This is my only night in town," I said artfully. "There's no telling when I'll see a woman again."

"But I'm not the only woman in Paris, you know," said she, still writing. "You'll have to take some of the other girls to-night."

Had she dropped a bomb on me I could not have been more unpleasantly surprised.

"But," I insisted, "there was something I wanted to ask you—something—very private."

"Ask it now," she said briskly, bending over another chart."

She could make me so happy and she wouldn't! Even her motherliness was gone. I suddenly began to hate her. I hated her crisp morning mood, her crisp, clear eyes, her crisp white skirt. I could have bitten my tongue out for dragging in an unwelcome personal note. But if I died for it I would finish.

"I wanted to know how you happened to be in Dublin," I said, very fast, "and why you looked at me as you did."

"Oh, that's it?" She wrote a few words. "Why, you see"—she paused abstractedly to fill in another line—"I was on leave before coming over here. So I went home to Ireland to see my brother who had been wounded. That's how it was."

Once more she was lost in a chart.

If I had asked a Wall Street broker on Monday morning to discuss Mrs. Browning's love sonnets, I could not have felt more calfish. But I meant to see it through.

"And the rest?" I set my teeth.

"Why—petrels have some points in common with swallows. Perhaps I clapped my beak in the masonic high-sign of birds. There was another reason I stared but I shan't tell that. You wouldn't like it. *Now*"—gathering up her papers she shook them into shape—"I must run. Come in and say good-bye before you go, won't you?"

"Yes," I murmured, moistening my lips.

"Be sure," she called, with a fleet smile over her shoulder.

I stumbled blindly into Foster's empty office and began to kick the furniture.

"Fool! Dolt! Ass!" I groaned, punctuating each word with a kick. "Poor prune! Poor prune!"

I had been on a two month's jag of egotism. The hang-over was a bad one. My brilliancy that I had recalled with complacency came back now in a duller light.

"I like you—why do you like me? You act about thirty——" Had I really said those things or was it a bad dream? And this morning, in the face of that cool, business-like greeting, I had snivelled sentimentally! I was burning up with shame for myself and rage at her crisp self-sufficiency. She had put me in my place. Well, I would stay put. I would *not* go to say good-bye.

"What's the matter with me, anyway, that I get stung every time?" I wondered.

Jumping up, I looked in a mirror. I tried to look impersonally.

Five feet eleven—not a giant, but not a dwarf; and I had always been proud of my shoulders. Muscles like steel springs, veins bubbling with vigorous blood, teeth sound and white, skin ruddy, eyes clear, hair on the jump but plenty of it—not bald, at any rate—and Mont Blanc sprouting lustily.

I turned from this inventory to meet Foster's laughing eye. But I was beyond caring.

"Foster," I began wildly, "do you consider me peculiarly repulsive to women?"

"You're crazy with the heat," said Foster calmly. "When did *you* come to town?"

"No, I'm not. I get on great with men but women!"

"Look here," said Foster earnestly, sitting down, "if you're still worrying about Myrtie or Migonette or Heliotrope or whatever her name was—forget it. There's plenty more fish in the sea—I've seen them flap their fins at you. There's just one thing about women—you have to knock 'em on the head. A touch of cave-man stuff does the work, my boy. They eat it up. And never let a woman know she's hooked you. Keep it dark, keep it dark."

My mind flew back to Shorty's prescription for spraying the little red mule's nose: "Rope her head—you gotta treat her as if she was a woman —rope her head!"

Without a word of excuse to Foster I tore out. All day I walked madly. "Keep it dark—knock 'em on the head." I repeated his words as if they were a ritual. "Cave-man stuff is what I hand out from now on. And I'll *not* go back to say good-bye."

At nine o'clock that night I found myself, for some reason unknown to myself, pacing up and down in front of her office. "And I'll *not* go in to say good-bye," I was murmuring. Mouth dry, eyeballs burning, pulse hopping—I was in best cave-man condition.

A door opened. A hand clutched my arm.

"You're an answer to prayer, Swallow! I haven't had a bite since breakfast—wait, wait!"

I was dashing out for a taxi.

"You must get me back by midnight. Promise not to fascinate me with tales of your misspent life till I forget to come home?"

"Keep it dark—knock 'em on the head," whispered the cave-man.

"I promise—anything," I said.

Leaning back in the car she closed her eyes. She was white and below her lashes were heavy shadows.

"You can't imagine," she said, lifting those lashes just enough to intoxicate me, "what heaven it is to have a man take care of you after taking care of men all day."

"Keep it dark—knock 'em on the head," prompted the cave-man.

"It's heaven—for me," I said.

Then speechless with gratitude for her presence I sat until we reached the café where we had been before. If I could only get our old table—that was the one important thing in life. Feverishly I besought the head waiter for it, and got it.

"Oh, how nice to be here again!" she exclaimed.

She had remembered!

"Yes, please, something hot. Spinach soup will be lovely. How that wine does revive one!"

There was a wine in my veins more potent than the life-blood of grapes. Wordless with contentment I watched the glow come back to her eyes.

"Isn't it lucky you hadn't dined?" she observed, dipping a spoon into the steaming soup. "Why hadn't you, by the way?"

"Keep it dark—knock 'em on the head," urged the cave-man.

"I couldn't eat," I said.

"Why not?" Her spoon was poised half-way to her mouth. Professional anxiety was in her tone.

"Keep it dark—knock 'em on the head," pleaded the cave-man.

"Because I thought you didn't like me this

morning," was what I said. I was horrified to hear a quaver in my voice.

"My *dear*—Swallow"—she dropped her spoon—"you're not—why, I had enough work to-day to turn seven saints into seven wild-cats —you're not——"

She looked at me helplessly.

"Yes, I am." Giving the cave-man a vigorous kick in the face I went desperately on. "I love you—everything about you——"

My voice broke.

"And you sat here not two months ago telling me—at this very table"—she tapped it with her little white hand—"that you would always love another girl! Blessed boy, where's your sense of humour?"

"But that wasn't——"

"Don't!" She laid her hand on mine. It was strong and mothering, not frail like Jasmine's. "Don't say that wasn't real love."

"Do they all say that?"

"Invariably."

"And does every man you meet tell you that he loves you?"

This seemed to me the obvious course for any man.

"Oh, *dear*, no," she said, horrified. "But you see, they aren't responsible, poor dears."

"And don't you want *me* to love you?" I asked, jealous of that plural.

"It wouldn't be fair if I did. You come in from the camp crazy to tell the first woman you meet about your girl. It's a glamorous subject and for the moment you think you're in love with the woman who listens to you. As soon as you're gone you know you weren't. You simply loved to talk to some one about love. That's what I mean when I say you're not responsible."

I thought hard. Then I said ponderously:

"If this is the regular procedure, why did you make me talk about my girl?"

For one startled second her eyes met mine. Then she laughed, that tonic laugh that I had not heard since Christmas night.

"Take me home," was her answer, "before you learn so fast that I can't like you any more for not understanding women."

This speech contained dizzy possibilities. I fed on it in the days to come. It was the most precious thing that I carried to camp.

*   *   *

In the new field I was given a big voisin with an inch cannon that fired a shell three thousand yards. We kept four machines over Paris. Each of us had to stay up two hours and a half every day at a height of six or ten thousand feet. It was disappointing but I never saw a Zeppelin. I never saw an airplane other than our own. I saw nothing but the domes and streets and trees of Paris all flattened down to the size of the Noah's Ark I had played with as a baby. Beyond the city I could see the fortifications; beyond those, the dim line of trenches. And never once did I fly over Paris but I tried to pick out the roof that covered her who was always in my thoughts. She was wrong, she was wrong! I had never really loved any but her. Some day I was going to make her believe it. And as I flew there so near her I was always rehearsing just how I would make her believe.

Soon I was put on the night patrol. The first night I was as high-strung as a race-horse. My nerves were snapping. It was the most intense moment of my life. With red and green lights tipping my wings I began to climb. I had no idea if I should ever come back. I could see the lights of Paris and sometimes a village road. I could tell the different aviation fields by the number of flashes they sent up. But suppose there should be a raid and all lights should be extinguished? Then I could only feel about through the darkness and pray that my motor would not fail me.

There was no raid. There was nothing worse than a cooling spark-plug that sent me limping home. Five times did the machine break on those night patrols. Five times I hobbled back, grazing the tree-tops as I came down. I could have landed in Paris; but I always took pride in getting back to the field.

My nerves grew tougher under the tension. But I never grew used to the loneliness—a loneliness that clamoured, a stillness that throbbed. Was *she* ever lonely, down there in the hospital?

Was she asleep, or out with some one luckier than I? Did she think of me ever? I was tied to field duty, but in fancy I was by her side.

All this time plans were going ahead for the American Squad. Our captain, like so many Frenchmen, was infatuated with America. When he learned of our intent he was determined to lead us. Because of my nationality then he took a special interest in me and went to great trouble to be pleasant to me. We exchanged French and English lessons. I grew to enjoy his grace of nature as much as I admired his rockribbed nobility. Indeed we became the warmest friends.

Once when his fiancée came out to visit him he asked me to dine with them. They frankly adored each other.

The captain had been flying a heavy machine. But to fit himself for leading the Americans he began to practice on the chassé. One day I watched him fly off in a little scout. He had not gone five hundred yards before he lost control, dropped into a spinning nose and crashed to earth.

Aroused by my cries nearly the whole camp ran to him. When I reached him some soldiers at work on a hill had pulled him out of the machine. He was lying with his head on a little mound of hay. With one hand at his wrist I tore open his shirt. I put my other hand at his heart. There was no life there. He gasped. The pulse in his neck gave one beat. He moved in my arms and died. I could not keep back the tears.

Then something happened which ever since has depressed me. The soldiers were kneeling with us at his side. One of them asked a comrade who had been a priest before the war to offer a prayer. "Is he a Christian?" the priest asked me. "Oui," I said. "Bien," he returned, and prayed.

Had my captain been a thief Christ would have blessed him. But he was a clean, upright man, who had given his life of love and splendid activity for a just cause. And this pitiful, small-souled priest must inquire his creed before giving his benediction.

A month after the captain's death the squad that he had hoped to lead was born. I received orders to report at the large depot of aviation in Belleville.

My precious last night in Paris could be spent in just one place, illumined by one presence. At our secluded table in the unsecluded café I sat flooded with the sure happiness that her nearness gave.

"I'm in earnest," I began.

"I'm not," she answered, a smile breaking her face up into little nooks.

"Won't you stop laughing long enough to tell me you know I love you?" I begged. I wanted from her own lips the assurance that my own were always hungering to give.

"For one minute I will be serious if you will frivol the rest of the evening. Agreed?" She help up a firm finger. "Well, then, there is only one way to know when love is real. That is when it can stand realities."

"What are realities?" I asked, ready to drag them in by the hair of their heads.

"One is time. One is sacrifice. There are moments, too, of suffering and danger that illuminate the heart, that make you know if you can bear delay and denial. And sometimes I think the greatest tests of all are success and happiness. Perhaps it's a greater tribute to need love when you're up than it is when you're down. Now, Swallow, time's up. Flap your wings and be merry!"

It was when I was leaving that I said quite suddenly:

"If I'm wounded will you save me a bed in your ward?"

Just as her smile had done when Foster had pledged my new pair of wings, her bright voice took one of those sudden drops into a strange, dark place. The eyes she lifted to mine held something I had never seen there before. Was it terror?

"Swallow," she said, "dear, unfledged Swallow, God grant I may never have the chance."

For a moment her look lingered in mine. I put out my hands to touch her. But she was gone.

After learning the little Nieuport at the depot I was sent to join the American Squad at Bar-le-Duc. At the town I was met by some of the older men. In our own motor they drove me to the field. There I found my own little Nieuport, our own mechanicians, rest tents, messengers, chauffeurs and a small army of other employées for our special edification. Halfway between the field and town was our villa with baths, conservatories, a grand piano, comfortable beds, and several cars. Nothing was too good for the Americans who had enlisted for France. Except when on guard, our time was our own. I thought exultantly now of that walk to Pau with a knapsack that rubbed my back and boots that blistered my feet. I contrasted that muddy, barren barrack with this princely comfort, those rigid rules with this elastic life. I was no longer a school-boy. I was a warrior!

The men I found here were as satisfying as the quarters—the finest brand of young Americans, I think, with the aviator blend of delicacy and daring.

Each of the squad had some special insignia for his machine. A member of the Hotfoot Club of Virginia had a printed foot, another an Indian head. Some used their own initials. With a remorseful thought for Jasmine back in Texas I painted on one side of my machine a huge star. On the other side less conspicuously I painted a tiny swallow.

Falling back to admire my creations I plumped smartly against another chap who, brush in hand, had stepped back for the same purpose. Looking around at the clap of meeting spines he saw my insignia.

"What'd you plagarise my planet for?" he demanded.

"I didn't plagarise your planet," I protested.

"You did," and he pointed to his own.

"Hey," called a third voice, "You two have a crust——coming out as the star of the squad! You'd better prove it first."

"Mine's the Lone Star of Texas," we chorused in unison. And finding we were fellow statemen we shook hands amicably.

My first flight over the lines was made under the wing of Dover Manley. Patrolling Dead Man's Hill, we kept a sharp lookout for machines bearing the black cross of Germany. As we found none we flew about awhile to watch the battle. It was the siege of Verdun and I had expected to see fierce fighting and hear the tremendous noise of war. I could hear nothing but the roar of my own motor. I could see nothing but a dishevelled strip of earth ploughed with mine craters. Back of the lines I did see something: on one side a little streak as if some one had scratched a match on the ground; on the other, little puffs of smoke like the dust from puff-balls. And that was all there was to the great battle of Verdun.

For some time my only taste of war was when I would drop into an immense hole in the air left by one of the big shells. And I was pining for a sight of the enemy. It came suddenly. A bomb burst just behind our hangar. The noise sickened me. I did not know what it was.

"A Boche, a Boche!" cried the boys.

Looking up I saw a bony white thing in the air, like the skeleton of a fish. It was a German machine!

My own machine was broken, but before I even thought of that, three of the chaps were up. A bomb dropped near me. My stomach caved in. Another bomb burst and another. Then a whistle blew. I began to run. Seeing a lot of workmen running, I joined them. I didn't know where they were going. I only knew I must get away from that noise.

Leaping over the ground, head down, I dove straight into the stomach of an officer.

"Where are you going?" he asked calmly.

I stopped and looked at him. War was here! The dream of my life was realised! And I, poor poltroon, was running away! Turning, I went with the officer to the town.

We counted over our heads fifteen machines.

Bar-le-Duc was in a valley. The railroad station was along the canal. Our field was on a plateau. Both field and station were easily seen from the air. Passing the station by entirely, dropping a few shells over the field by way of pastime, the Germans deliberately bombed the town—bombed peaceful old men and women and children.

The invasion of Belgium was evidence enough that Germany had no more sense of civilisation than a savage. I had heard first-hand a hundred instances of barbarous treachery. I knew the English doctor who had responded to the call of a wounded German on the field and who after caring for the man as if he were one of his own countrymen, was shot in the back by his patient. I knew a dozen more men who themselves had experienced the brutal breaking of every war condition to which Germany had pledged itself. But not till my own eyes saw these crumpled homes of innocent civilians, women without faces, old men without arms and legs, babies without mothers—not till now did I know why I was fight-

ing. My adventure was now an adventure of
purpose.

Next day my machine was in order so that I was
able to fly with the others. It was much less terrifying to be in the air firing a machine gun than
to stand on the earth below, where all effort was
absolutely useless. It made me realise more poig-
nantly the outrage against those old men and
women.

Our boys did what they could but the Germans
had the advantage. In the air one must work
on three dimensions instead of two: width, breadth
and height. Distances, of course, are enormous.
If a German is five or six hundred yards away and
happens to have a speedy machine, a gun is useless. The point of vantage is from above with
the sun at your back so if the enemy looks in your
direction he can not see you. The Germans now,
of course, could climb high and we were at a dis-
advantage.

Day after day they bombed us. Just as we would
settle down to a noon beefsteak, would come the
cry: "Les Boches!" Out we would run. "My
trousseau, Antoinette!" I would call to Anton,
my mechanician. Then not waiting for it I would
cram down my cap, jump in the car, shout "Contact!" and fly off. Four times a day I would go

to a height of five thousand yards. It was a terrific strain and useless. Not till they had bombarded us a week did I get from my machine a glimpse of the enemy.

That day, just as I left the ground, I saw twelve German machines, all from two to three thousand metres up. Setting my machine at a tangent, I started climbing. Around and around under the Germans I circled. Looking down at the town, I saw little brown puffs of smoke from the German bombs. Looking up at the Germans I saw little puffs of white smoke from the French shells.

I was halfway between the two. It seemed safer to get close up under the Germans; so I started climbing. By the time I reached their height they had all disappeared except one little scout. I was right in under him. I went on climbing. So did the scout. The faster I climbed the faster he climbed. Try as I would I could not get ahead of him.

"Pt!" He was firing at me.

Dropping my machine down into a reloading position, I fired back.

"Pt!" answered he.

"Pt!" rejoined I.

"Pt, pt, pt!" he sputtered.

"Pt, pt, pt yourself," I retorted.

This last word came high. I had spent my last cartridge! If he fired again and I did not answer he would know he had me. But happily he disappeared behind the German lines and I scudded back to the field. That was the last day of the bombardment.

I liked best my flights with Dover Manley. I had for him the admiration of a cub for a master flier and the admiration of every one who knew him for a high-hearted soldier. In an older brother way Dover took great pains with me—trimmed me off, watered me down, patted me into shape.

His only fault as an aviator was an excess of bravery. He never left a German until he was sure he had driven him out of control. He used to come back with bullet holes in his sleeve or his shoe. His machine, with the fifty odd patches where it had been struck, looked like a crazy-quilt. Once, absorbed in a fight with a German, he failed to observe a Fokker over him till the pilot dove on him, caught him in his line of fire, riddled his machine, broke the main control, cut through his head-guard and opened up his scalp. Catching hold of the two broken ends of the control, Dover flew home. His wounds were dressed without his going to a hospital. His machine was repaired immediately. And the next day Dover was back on the German lines.

One day we had started out together when indistinctly through the mist I saw a German. Making a short turn I dove on him, but before I could reach him Dover was on his tail. Hoping to help Dover I tried to follow them. I lost sight of them both, but every time I heard Dover's mitrailleuse, I went after it. Soon the popping ceased. Through the silence and the mist I flew about trying to locate Dover. Suddenly I saw him peering at me from a cloud. We flew home together. When we landed Dover told me that he had gone down on his nose out of control and had lost his man.

"And I want to tell you, kid, you're the real stuff," he said, stripping off his Teddy-bear garments. "When a fellow hears something that he thinks is a Boche and finds a friend instead, it's a happy surprise party."

Another morning about four o'clock on patrol, my machine balked. As the fellows were several hundred yards above me, I could not reach their altitude. Suddenly my tail went up. I sat down hard in a hollow of air. Then beside me I heard a big "Chou!" I could see nothing. It was like

a giant spitting out of invisibility. In a second
I heard another "Chou!" This time I saw beside me a puff of grey smoke. The German anti-
aircraft guns were after me! Now the shells were
all around me. One nipped off a wing. Another
smashed the mirror in front of me.

"It's up and out of this for you, quick, my boy,"
I thought. As fast as I could I veered off to the
left. Coming out of its early morning grouch just
in time, my machine began to climb again. In
two minutes I was safe at several hundred yards
above our boys. But I came back from that ex-
pedition with the sense of occupying a prominent
place in the thoughts of the German army. In a
trench you have no identity. A shell is fired not
at you but at a hundred. In aërial combat there is
more personal feeling. You and your German,
alone in the world, are fighting. But when you
are the sole target of the anti-aircraft guns, when
five or six complete batteries are aiming intimate
messages of spite from Germany to you—then do
you feel that you occupy a large area on the map
of war. And with deep thankfulness I saw the
home field that day.

The return was always warmly satisfying, anyway. The exultancy of flying takes a heavy toll
in nervous tension. The isolation is a strain.

Death is imminent. And to come back to the substantial earth, to secure human contacts, brought the glow that follows hazardous enterprise. If one came home with a Boche to his credit the satisfaction was doubled. That was a triumph I never had a chance to taste.

We were required to make two patrols a day over the Verdun lines. Each patrol lasted from two to three hours. What other flying we did was voluntary.

These were stirring days, with the hardest strain, the keenest reward that I had ever known. We were called early in the dark of the morning. After an unceremonious cup of coffee we would motor to the field. While we donned our "trousseaus" the mechanicians rolled the machine from the hangars. Then the shriek of "Contact!" from the man below and before the answering shriek was fairly from our mouths, it seemed, we were four thousand feet up.

As dawn began to smudge the east with pink we could see a cluster of red roofs, a strip of broken earth, pillars of dark smoke, showers of shells. That was the Battle of Verdun.

Back for a brief rest in the tent before lunch, then another sortie. After the second breathing-spell some of us would voluntarily make a third trip. By that time we had keen appetites for dinner in the villa where we messed with our officers.

I shall never forget my last night at the villa. After a devastating game of poker, I wandered into the music-room. The captain at the grand piano was softly playing Debussey. From behind a closed door the phonograph was shrieking "The Saucy Little Bird on Nelly's Hat." It was a chilly June night and a bunch of the boys, lounging about the open fire, were talking in low tones on subjects seldom discussed in that healthy, objective spot—the intimate subjects of love and marriage, religion and death.

Throwing myself down into a deep chair beyond the firelight, I thought of the girl in Paris —in Paris no longer. No, she was not there tonight. She had written me that she was going to the front on a special mission for a few days. I knew what "special mission" meant and all day at the thought of her my heart had pounded in terror. Now, however, a strange hush had come over my whole spirit. I was no longer afraid for her. I was glad that she, as well as I, was a part of it all. I was glad for the things she could bring to a world of suffering—the merry smile, the wide heart, the tender Irish eyes.

"My girl," I said to myself, "my girl, my girl! If you knew how I felt about you, you'd believe!"

CHAPTER V

IT was dawn, June 18, 1916. Four of us left the field to make our regular patrol. Each was in his own machine—the captain, Payne, King and I. Flying together in a flock we patrolled the whole Verdun front, across Hill No. 304, then turned and started home.

We were still well back within German territory when underneath me I saw a German. Farther down over Hill No. 304 I saw more Germans and dimly through the mist still more Germans.

Payne and King were flying together at my right. Pulling up closer to the captain I wigwagged my machine. From that he would know I had discovered an enemy. Then I began to watch my man. Soon I saw him separate from the others. It looked like a good chance to get on him unawares.

"If I miss him," I thought, "I'll fly right on home, then come back again."

I kept one eye on the captain. He had inclined his plane. Evidently he was going after one of the other Germans whose presence I had signalled him.

Making a sharp turn so as to get my man in the path of fire, I dove as steeply as possible. As I came down I saw that his machine was small—possibly a two-seater. That meant that he was as fast as I. One second I poised for decision. In that second lay my future. I decided to attack.

I ran up to him. I passed. He crossed my line of fire. I opened up my gun. He dropped into my sights. I fired—once, twice. Those were my first and last shots. My machine gun had jammed!

Now the other Germans began to appear through the mist. One was at my left, two were on my right, one was underneath, the man I had first attacked was behind me. From the silence of my gun they would know there was nothing to fear. They would get on top of me. My fight was over. I was too far behind the German lines to dive to earth. I could only manœuvre back to the field.

I began to loop; I swung in every direction; I went into a cloud. Bullets followed.

"Pt!" One had scratched my machine.

I slipped away from the man who fired it and threw the belly of my plane upwards.

"Pt, pt, pt!" This time one went through.

"Pt, pt, pt! Pt, pt, pt! Pt, pt, pt!" The machine was full of them.

I was now about twelve thousand feet up. It was while I was standing completely on my head, the belly of my plane skyward, that something struck me. It felt like the kick of a mule. I had the sensation of losing a leg and put my hand down to learn if I were all there. I was strapped in too tightly to be knocked overboard and I had the presence of mind to cut the motor. But as my right foot went back with the shock of the bullet, my left foot sprang forward. So with my commands reversed, my leg out of business, still standing on my head, I fell into a spinning nose dive.

Around and down, around and down. It was all over. Soon I should hit the ground as I had seen so many friends hit it. That would be all. How strange that I, the I that had seemed undying, should hit the ground like all the rest. I remembered the first man I had picked up. I should look like that. I remembered when I had picked up my captain. I had cried. Would any one cry for me? Would the girl in Paris care?

Around and down—why, could this be death, this ease—almost this ecstasy—of giving up? There was no terror, no numbness; nothing but my clear mind following my body—following, not fighting. Why, death could not be like this! I must see her again, the Stormy Petrel. That thought came thundering through space. Came a second crash—France, my usefulness, my job. I was giving these without a struggle.

"Stop yourself, coward!"—I was shouting it out loud, trying to shout it above this rush of air that had been drugging me into abandonment. "You're not dead. Don't be a quitter. Mother —don't let me give up! Mother!"

Before that moment I had been a boy, adventurous, enthusiastic, perhaps as courageous as the most. To me at twenty, flying for France had been sport, well-meant, timely, even gallant, but still sport. It was not until I flung my mother's name into the drowning air that I crossed the line between sport and conflict. In that second I grew up.

Making a supreme effort, I tried to push my bad leg with my hand; but the machine planes were so wedged in the fall that I could not get the commands. If I hit here I should be a German prisoner. Working my right leg with my hands, working it desperately, at last I felt the kinks come out of the commands. Once more the machine was on the level. Now if I could make my dazed brain remember the rules for flying with one foot. Pull the left instead of pushing with the right—if I could remember to do that!

"Pt, pt, pt!"

My gun was still useless. My entire right side was paralysed. I was bleeding like a pig. But at that sound I dove again. This time I kept control. I was low enough now so that through the mist I could see the trenches like worm-eaten wood, and the snaky curve of the river. I put my plane in more than a vertical dive, shooting back under the Germans so far that the roll of cartridges fell out and falling, hit my arm. I thought I had been struck again. Everything was falling out now.

"Pt, pt, pt!"

I looked at my metre. Eight hundred feet above ground. I was going to hit in Germany!

I could see the trenches. I must get home! Pulling back the release I opend up the motor. It was now making fifteen hundred revolutions a minute; it could go no faster. I poised a second, then took a long running dive over the lines. I went so fast that I could scarcely recognise the trenches. I went so far that I left my enemies out of sight.

I was now growing too faint to go on. I saw

a green field and, making a turn to the left, came up to the wind and dove for the field. Too late I saw that it was filled with barbed wire; I was landing between the front line trenches and the reserve lines. The barbed wire caught my wheels and very gently my machine turned completely upside down. I knew that it was going over me. I should bleed to death after all. But as it turned my straps tore loose. The belt that held me dropped me, alive, in France, with my machine safe beside me.

Pain left me, fear left me. Was this helpless safety the thing for which I had fought my spiritual battle up there in the air?

Safety? In the field next to me I saw a burst of smoke, then a white spot; then another and another before I realised what it meant. The Germans were shelling me from the air. They had seen me fall; they were trying to kill me where I lay; worse yet, they were trying to destroy my machine.

"Cowards!" I cried, "to hit a machine when it's down!"

I was sure I said the words aloud, yet I could not hear them. Now I knew why I did not hear the bombs they were firing at me; my ears had been deadened by the terrific fall. It was like the movies, to watch the thunderous shells burst silently near me.

When the bombing stopped, some one would come for me. I suffered so little pain that I knew I was not badly wounded. I should be sent to Paris. The Stormy Petrel would take care of me; she had promised. Then when I was getting well we would have more gay little dinners; her eyes would laugh at me across the table, laugh away something deeper than laughter. Then I would come back to the squad and fight, and the next time I would get my German. But, strange climax of the human heart, now, after that victory over myself, it was more of those good times in Paris that I thought than of my job.

The bursts of smoke had ceased. Tired of waiting, I tried to crawl. I could not move. I got up on my hands and knees to try again but could no more move than if I had been staked to the ground. Finally, catching the grass, I dragged myself like a dog with a broken back. Inch by inch I made about ten yards; then I could go no farther.

It was now about six o'clock in the morning. The sun which had driven away the mist, flamed down upon me in the unshadowed field. I unbuttoned my heavy flying clothes. I took the shoe off my right foot; it dripped red. Utterly exhausted by these efforts, I could feel only a dumb wonder at the sight. Somehow I could not connect that bleeding foot with myself. I was all right. I must let my mother know this at once. Then I would go to Paris for those good times.

After I had waited a few minutes longer, four French soldiers came, stooping low; they, too, had kept quiet till the shelling had ceased. Crawling under the barbed wire, they caught hold of me and asked what was the matter.

"Bullet—in my—hip," I muttered, choking back with each word a groan at the touch of their hands. The pain of their rough grasp was so severe that now for the first time I wondered. Could my wound be worse than I had thought?

"Can you walk?" they asked in French.

"*Mais non,*" said I, indignantly.

Two took me by the shoulders, two by the feet. Then like a beast unleashed my pain broke from its long stupor. Almost crawling to escape the enemy's eye, the four men dragged me like a sack of grain. Through the long grass, over and across and under the web of barbed wire, my bleeding body sagged and sometimes bumped the ground. The pain had now become such torture that I almost fainted. Oh, if only some enemy *would* see us, would shoot an end to my hell!

I do not know how long that journey lasted. All I do know is that at last we came to the dressing-station behind the trenches. Here, lying face downwards on a bed, I thought of only one thing. As a child longs for home at night, I longed for mine. The rattle of the poker-chips, a big American voice singing "You Made Me Love You"—American ragtime, jokes, faces—if I could only get back to these to-day, it didn't matter where that German bullet hit. Then to-morrow I should see the girl. The boys would send me to Paris.

Meanwhile some one was pulling off my fur combination. As they cut away my shirt and dressed the wound, the antitoxin numbed the pain. Now I suffered no more than I had there on the field. It was in this deadened state that, looking around, I saw for the first time the hole in my hip. With a curiosity that was almost grotesque, I stared at that wound. All the time it seemed to me that this gaping, black hole belonged to some other man; just as when I had looked at my bleeding foot I could not believe it was mine.

The stretcher-bearers were making ready to pick me up. I looked at them beseechingly.

"To my squad at Bar-le-Duc—right away—please," I begged.

They made no reply, and carrying me face downward, my fur coat thrown over me, through an·underground trench, they placed me at last on the floor of the *poste de secours*. As I lay there waiting my turn for the ambulance, I watched three other men go out before me. Again came the intense incredulity. Was it really I waiting so helplessly, or was it one of those men I carried when I drove an ambulance?

"To my squad at Bar-le-Duc—right away—please," I repeated to the broad-shouldered young man preparing to lift me to his ambulance. He, like the stretcher-bearer, did not answer. I looked into the dark, triangular face bending over me and clenched my teeth in a fury of futile homelessness.

"One moment here!"

A man who had just jumped from a car hurried into the little station and held up his gloved hand for attention.

"Is there an aviator here who fell a few hours ago?"

"I—right here," I answered eagerly.

"*Oui, oui*, I saw your fall. I am a member of the reconaissance squad. My car is at your disposal."

I could have cried out with joy. The fat little Frenchman, with his red point of beard and reddish brown eyes, took on the glorified aspect of a deliverer. I could not thank him enough.

"*Merci, merci, merci!*" I exclaimed. "*Je suis un Americain, Lafayette Escadrille, Bar-le-Duc. Toute de suite, s'il vous plait.*"

"*Bien, bien,*" said he, calling his driver to help lift me from the floor.

With the fur coat still thrown over me, my stretcher was placed across the front and back of the opening in the touring car. As the driver settled himself at the wheel, my new friend seated himself to hold the stretcher in place. Just as we were ready the chief of the station came out to the car.

"To V——," he ordered in a loud tone. "V—— is only twenty miles. Bar-le-Duc is thirty. This man is not able to travel so far. To V——!"

There was complete finality in his tone. Yet despite this and my present sickening disappointment, I still held fast to my purpose. If they would not take me to my friends, I would have

my friends send for me. For I must see the
nurse to-morrow. All through that long, torturing drive over one of the roughest roads in
France my thoughts crowded about those moments
of homecoming. This drive, scarcely bearable in
an ambulance, was almost unsupportable in a
light car that permitted my stretcher to jerk back
and forth. Every time we went down into a shell-
hole I could hardly keep from screaming. My
captain, the boys—to-night; my nurse—to-morrow. That intense thought became a prayer.

At last we reached V——. Here I was carried
into a long, narrow shed packed tightly with other
men on stretchers like myself. By this time I was
half fainting. Perhaps because of this the first
sight of the shed had the stagnant horror of a
dream. As an ambulance driver I was used to
such scenes, but then I had been well. Now each
mutilated form caught up my own suffering, repeated it, dinned it into my brain, until I thought
I had never known health or peace or beauty.

I looked around me in terror. Mud was thick
on the floor. Flies came down like droves of lo-
custs. The stench was that of a stock-yard.
Poilus, some with arms torn off, some with heads
half shot away, shouted like madmen.

My driver was leaving me now. As he put me down I made a groping movement for his arm.

"Thank you, and for God's sake," I said—"for God's sake telephone my captain at Bar-le-Duc to come for me to-day."

He promised, but as he turned away a man started to undress me.

"Don't take off my clothes," I commanded. "I am leaving here in a few moments."

He paid no attention.

"I forbid you to take off my clothes," I screamed. "I am an American; I am going to my squad."

He made no answer. Instead, from the *Poilu* next to me came a cry that tore the air. I closed my eyes to shut out the scene. When I opened them again a surgeon was standing over me.

"I'll just look at the wound," said he. "If I can get the bullet out you can go on to your friends this afternoon."

Reassured, I let them take off my clothes. Then, naked and partly paralysed, I lay on the dirty canvas stretcher with a blanket thrown over me until I was carried to a table in the little white-washed shed that served as an examination room. With a radioscope under my body the doctor marked me six or seven times.

"Only one bullet?" he asked.

"Yes," said I.

"I don't believe it hit the bone, but I'll have to take it out. Then you can go to your friends to-morrow."

To-morrow! I must be in Paris to-morrow! Oh, I never could wait till to-morrow to go to Bar-le-Duc!

I waited a year.

They carried me to a table in the operating shed. The last thing I saw was the doctor's apron, a solid crimson patch. Then struggling little, breathing easily, I swam out across the breakers into a shining calm that spread and spread and carried me on a joyous rosy tide to Paris.

I awoke at noon, not in Paris, but on a stretcher. Through my twilit senses I could dimly see my captain.

"*Mon capitaine,*" I cried. "It wasn't my fault. My machine-gun jammed. I fired at him once but my gun broke."

"It's all right, my little one, it's all right."

The light stinging French accents of my officer seemed to prick the darkness about me. I wondered if they were fireflies. I dropped asleep. At evening I awoke, begging for water. Some one shot some dope into me and I went back into a hot darkness that lasted until morning. Again I awoke, begging for water. More hot darkness. I struggled through black suffocation. I pulled one leg after the other toward an icy mountain brook that laughed hilariously as it hurried to the sea. How easy for it to run, how hard for me! I strained each leg up from the steaming swamp but could never get ahead. Summoning all my will, I awoke with the cry of "Water!"

Some one brought me a bit of wet bandage to suck. There was a violent numbness in my hip; weakness and thirst were all I suffered now. With my wounded leg drawn up and my knee doubled tight, I could turn on one side. For the first time I had a chance to survey my surroundings.

Ten miles back from the Verdun front, the great French evacuation hospital where I lay was near enough for German aeroplanes to bomb us frequently. Indeed, the hospital was intended merely for operation; as soon as a man was able to be moved he was sent to Paris or elsewhere for treatment. The average patient stayed three days; a few bad cases stayed five.

As an aviator I had been given the best the hospital afforded. I was in the officers' ward, a long shed packed tightly with thirty cots. Made of three pine boards covered with a straw mattress, two coarse sheets, a small pillow and blankets, these beds were very different from those we now give our wounded. Then, at the height of the Verdun siege, every bed was filled. In fact during my whole stay I never saw an empty one.

As I looked down over the rows of beds I again had the feeling that life was echoing unbearably my own state. There in the receiving room it had been the torment of pain that had been caught up and dinned into my brain by those poor *Poilus*. Now in these dumb eyes about me I saw my own drugged and stricken will.

It was toward one person they were all looking. Irresistibly I followed their gaze. Madame, chief of the five women nurses, was just coming in from the dressing-room. Her skirt was like a snowy sail, and on her sleeve I caught the gleaming cross of the *Secours des Blesses*. There was dauntless energy in that profile, which in its bold curve reminded me of the prow of a boat.

Yet it was more than courage that took her to duty under fire. Tenderness was back of the dauntless profile—tenderness that made her eyes give a separate look to each of those thirty men. It was a gift, that swift enfolding glance, and as I received my own I knew why they all turned to her so hungrily. She was more than a nurse, more than a woman; she was a presence. Every time she glided into the room she seemed to each man there like a long-awaited ship from home.

In the days that followed I don't know what I should have done without Madame. When she was away I used to long for her to come back into the room. Even her French had a homey sound, and the crooning little way she had of saying *"Mon fils"* made me feel as if I were back with my own mother in Texas.

Of course we saw very little of her. For all those fifty portable houses that constituted the hospital, there were only five women. The rest of our nurses were young medical students who would have been graduated in 1917. They had intended to go on with their medical training in the auxiliary army, but having for various reasons been found unfit for service, had been transferred to the medical ward. Despite their medical training, the most of these students had none of the sick-room efficiency instinctive in the average untrained woman. True, they would doubtless have done better had they not been overworked. But there were not enough nurses, either men or women, to give us more than the most meagre care.

A few moments after Madame entered the room

that first morning the surgeon who had operated on me came striding down to my bed.

"Ah, ha, boy," said he, holding up to me a little bag, "I'll show you what I got out of *you*—six pieces of bullet. Want them for a souvenir?"

Strange how lively is the grim humour of the hospital! To the outside world it might seem strange, these jokes made by dying men. To us it seemed to me we were always waiting for a chance to laugh. For instance, a short time after my arrival I heard a young officer saying peevishly to his surgeon: "Why didn't you bring me all the *bone* you got out of my hip? You might have known this wouldn't be enough to make dice."

Now as I looked up at the bullets that had brought me here I felt myself grinning. My own enjoyment was echoed by a grizzled old major, who, brought in yesterday at the same time I was, lay in the bed next to mine. Painfully wounded as he was he gave a little crow when I put the bullets down on the stand at the head of my bed.

"Well, Doc," said I, staring up into the surgeon's sun-filled brown eyes and brown, sun-streaked face, "what time am I leaving to-day?"

He was an attractive chap in a lean, feline way

and there was real kindliness in the look he turned down to me.

"Not to-day, my little one; to-morrow, perhaps. There are many more pieces of this bullet to follow. It was explosive, you know."

Blankly, unbelievingly, I stared up into his face.

"Never mind," said he, answering the disappointment of my glance, "I'll give you something you'll like as well as a trip to Bar-le-Duc," and he pulled out his hypodermic.

For a while a wide, floating joy, then another fall into the hot swamp. I was hip-deep in black ooze. Mosquitoes as large as my own aeroplane buzzed about my head. I clutched at the underbrush that smothered me, trying to pull myself up by it. It was devil's-club. My hand was full of thorns. Before me the mountain-stream hurried to the sea. It tossed white arms in the air. It looked back at me over its shoulder with a mocking smile in its cool, blue eyes.

"Now, altogether, boys! Pull—pull out of this!" I commanded.

My eyes jerked open. I knew now what it was I had been trying to pull out of. It was thirst, more intolerable than anything I had ever felt. Compared with this agony my previous state had been only a wish. Now the cry for water was so intense that it absorbed every other sense. I wanted to hear water, to see water, to feel it trickling through my fingers. So violent was this one longing that I was actually blinded. I did not at first see a man standing beside my bed.

They came to me one by one—the heavy black hair, the great arms, and the sincerest eyes in the world. When I put them all together I gave a groan of joy. It was Dover Manley, flown over from Bar-le-Duc.

"Hello, old boy," he was saying, "here's your tooth-brush."

He was holding it out in his great paw, and I think I realised even then how hard he was trying to be matter of fact. The tooth-brush, the English words, the dear American voice, the aviator whom every one in our squad loved deeply— I knew nothing now except that I had them again. Then in a moment it came back to me, the terrible thirst. "Oh," I thought with a touch of the craftiness that is part of sickness, "if I can only *look* how thirsty I am, Dove will do something about it. He'll see that I get something better than an old wet bandage to suck."

"Anything I can get for you, old man?" said he, meeting my thirsty eyes.

"You bet," said I. "They won't let me have any water."

The way I kept moistening my lips finished the appeal.

"How about oranges?" said he, and turned to my doctor, just that moment come in.

"*Bien*," answered the surgeon with a shrug, "but there are not any to be had in the village."

"Guess we'll fix that," said Dover. "I'll get you those oranges if I have to fly to Paris."

I looked from one to the other. Oranges! Why hadn't I thought of those before? There is a certain sublime ignominy in the way a sick man permits himself to gloat over something he cannot have. I gave myself up to this ignominy completely.

"Dontchu worry," said Dover, lingering by my side and giving my arm a bear-like pat. "Be out of this in no time."

He was part of my beloved Bar-le-Duc. He was my friend in a world of strangers, yet I looked at him almost impatiently. When would he leave to get the oranges?

The next morning I woke from my hot, drugged sleep to find my captain bending over me.

"Well, my little one," said he, "I have a present for you."

Could it be the oranges at last? I looked up expectantly.

Something in the expression of my officer's face drew my attention to the whole room. There was a deep hush and through it I felt the eye of every man upon me. Then I saw for the first time that my captain was not alone. The major and colonel were with him.

Suddenly the colonel stepped forward.

"In the name of the republic," began he—he took from his pocket a large box—"I confer upon you *le Medaille Militaire* and *la Croix de Guerre.*"

"For me?" I asked in surprise. "What for?"

The figure in its horizon-blue gathered as if about to spring.

"*Pourquoi?*" His light, racing syllables slowed solemnly. "You are the first American aviator to be severely wounded—for France. With marvellous calmness of mind, suffering greatly as you must have suffered, you flew far, far, far over German ground to bring your machine back safe—to France. There is sometimes a braver thing than overcoming an enemy. It is overcoming yourself. You, my son, have done this—for a country not your own."

He bent down and kissed me on both cheeks.

Then, as I wore no shirt, he laid the medals on the pillow beside me.

My physical combat had been useless. My spiritual combat had resulted in my one real service. My only value to France had been exactly the value of the machine I had brought home. From my decision to stay on the job had sprung my one bit of usefulness; for that decision had come now these small honours. Had I but known it, this was a symbol of my future. It justified the instinct that later kept me on the job when I could see no chance for serving, no chance for being anything but a burden. How strange that this cool, efficient colonel should have commended my struggle rather than my performance! No, not strange. That was the spirit of his country.

In the solemn hush a cork popped. Madame had produced some champagne and was pouring a little in the glass of every man in the ward.

"*Vive le petit américain!*" she proposed, her soft eyes, as mellow and lively as the wine, smiling at me over the bottle.

"*Vive le petit américain!*" came back the cheers, some almost a bark of pain, some already feeble with death, as those grizzly spectres raised themselves on their pillows.

Ah, now I knew what it all meant—those people grouped about me like the picture of some famous death-bed. Yesterday I had seen two men decorated. Both had died within the hour. So my time had come!

"*Merci*," I responded in a scared voice. Then to my own surprise I heard myself adding firmly, "But I'm not going to die."

Why did I say this? Only a moment before, all morning, all through the fitful torments of the night, the courage to live had been slowly leaving me. This weakness, which made my body stretch into miles of weariness, each mile dwindling into a thinner thread; this thirst, which filled my mind to madness—now indeed life was a harder thing than it had seemed up there in the air. That fight had meant only a tremendous quickening. This, I was beginning to see, was a slow resolution which must pit itself minute by minute and hour by hour against a torture of weakness and thirst. The colonel's words of a moment before came back to me. I *would* get well!

The ceremony was over. The officers had congratulated me and left. Lying back, I looked at my insignia on the pillow beside me. My mother —I wanted her to see those bits of ribbon and metal. My eyes dimmed. The nurse in Paris— I wanted her to know. For one moment I thrilled.

As I looked, however, I had a sudden wayward thought. If only those medals were oranges! I thought of oranges I had seen in California groves, compact balls of sunshine among their dark leaves; of whole boxes of oranges tilted up temptingly in fruit-stands; of sliced oranges dripping with nectar as I had eaten them in Paris cafés. If I could only melt those medals and drink them from a glass—melt them into cold, fragrant, golden juice——

"Boy." I heard the old major who lay next to me addressing me sharply.

I looked up and saw that he had raised himself on his pillow. There was a fierce interrogation in his eyes that made me quail. Had he read my sacrilegious thought?

"Do you understand what it means—that which has just happened to you?" he was saying now.

"*Oui,*" I murmured.

"To fight for France, to die for France—it is a privilege given only to a few. You, boy, are one of those few. Do you comprehend, then, the honour of your lot?"

Utterly exhausted, he fell back to his pillow, but his eyes, still fixed upon me, had in them so holy and deathless a joy that my soul was awed before it.

I stammered that I did appreciate it. I made a giant effort to put away all thought of my thirst, and on some bits of paper I had found began writing to my mother. "Don't worry. I am going to get well." No one will ever know what it cost me to write those few words. Yet, spurred on by the old major, I made myself write still another line. Then, completely prostrated, I laid the scraps down, and to keep them from blowing away, held them on the table by my bag of bullets. It took many days of real toil to finish that letter.

Next day the oranges did come. But it was not Dover Manley who brought them. It was Payne who thrust the bag into my hand.

I did not at first ask why this was. With my eyes fixed on that golden hoard of fruit, I almost trembled to begin. But my old major. He must see no such greed. I waited until every man in the ward was supplied before I myself claimed my guerdon. It was only after a few rapt swallows of the cooling juice that I remembered to ask about Dover.

"Couldn't come to-day; machine's busted," replied Payne, leaving me somewhat abruptly. "One of the boys will get you some more tomorrow."

The next day a young French officer looked up at me suddenly from his Paris paper. *"Connais-sez-vois un américain,* Dover Manley?" asked he.

"Oui, oui, oui!"

"Il est mort."

"Mais non!"

"Mais oui! Voilà!"

He then showed me the clipping. Killed in an air-fight with a Boche while on his way with oranges for a sick friend at the hospital in V——! I could not keep back a cry. The next orange that I tried choked me. Yet a few hours afterwards I was goaded by my thirst into taking another swallow. After that, morning, noon and night, I held an orange to my lips. It was to me at first a kind of ferocious contradiction. It pressed in more bitterly the real grief for my friend at the same time that it released all the physical longing of my body. Gradually, however, I forgot everything else in the heaven of its fruity sweetness.

By this time I no longer thought of going to Bar-le-Duc. My desire was concerned only with the girl in the hospital at Paris. To-morrow I should go, the doctor kept promising; yes, absolutely, I should be moved to-morrow. And when Foster came down to see me once I said, "There was a little joke with Miss Gale—she was to keep a bed for me in her ward. Tell her now it's not a joke any longer—I'll be there to-morrow."

But on the fourth day the shifting to-morrow vanished. Then it was that an orderly carried me the length of the ward to the dressing-table. For the first time since my arrival the wound was to be dressed.

As the doctor ripped the packing from the wound, I heard a splash on the floor. I looked around to see what had fallen. Dirty corrugated blood rolled out by the cupful. I looked around again and saw a hole in my body like a large open box.

"What'd you cut me up so for, Doc?" I asked in a frightened voice.

"I had to, my little one."

"But how am I going to get to Paris to-day with that hole in me?" I asked faintly.

"Oh, in ten days you get there."

Ten days! And every day he had been saying to-morrow! Was my wound so much worse? I looked up at him with scared questioning.

"*Voilà!*" he was saying merrily. "I pack that hole in you like a pony-pack and strap you up tight like a bellyband. Then you gallop back to bed."

All the time that he was fixing me up I kept my eyes on his face. There was still frightened questioning in the look. I had never realised before that my wound was a serious one. At last I opened my lips. I wanted to ask him something. At this moment, however, an orderly seized me, spilled me into bed and hurried on to another patient. No one person could get much time in the hospital at V——.

It was the day after this, the fifth day of my residence at V——, that they first gave me water —water with vichy. In the meanwhile I had begun to suffer for the food which, because my intestines were pierced in a dozen or more places, they had not yet permitted me. Now indeed, the longest, bitterest hour of the day was at noon. Then the other men were eating. I could smell those savoury French soups. I could see those airy French omelettes, but I could never have a taste.

"*Garcon*, what shall I have for luncheon?" I would say to the orderly; "*Sole Marguery*, perhaps, and sauterne?"

He was a supple, slim-waisted young Frenchman, with tiny black eyes, like a mouse's, which almost met over his long, mouse-like nose; the whitest, the most perfect teeth I have ever seen; and the smile of a hyena. His smile held a shud-

dering fascination for me. I would try to call it
out; then, panic-stricken at the sight, try to push
it back.

"I'll bring you a dish, Monsieur, that is to-day's
specialty," he would reply before he hurried off,
to return with a long rubber tube twisted over his
arm like a rhythmic napkin. He would then jab
in his hypodermic needle, pour in a quart of saline
solution, and announce with savage obsequious-
ness, "Luncheon is served."

At the point of the needle my skin would puff
out as big as two fists, and my heart would pump
the life-giving fluid through my veins.

"You have excellent assimilation, Monsieur,"
the orderly would comment with that dreaded
flash of white teeth. "*Voilà*, how quickly you di-
gest your luncheon!"

Then came the day when I banqueted on milk
and vichy, and finally the day the doctor had set
for my release, the day when I first had coffee.

Coffee was salvation. There was the long, hot
purgatory of night, when the lights were dimmed,
when windows and doors were shut tightly against
bombing Germans, when the stench of thirty
wounded men, unwashed for weeks, was that
of a dog-kennel, when every second was a century.
Then morning, the wonder how you were to live

through the sleepless day, the end of your endurance and—coffee! For days I had watched other men find revival in that steaming cup. Now my turn had come.

The first gulp brought a hopeful sense of vigour I had nôt known since I was hurt. Excited by the stimulant, exultant over my coming freedom, I lay upon the surgeon's table waiting to have my wound dressed.

"Well, Doc," was the way I reminded him of his promise, "what would you say if I'd run up to town to-day and have a little spree?"

He looked down at me with his warm, childlike eyes.

"Would you rather be patient here a little longer and get well, or die to-night on the way to Paris?"

Under the feeding of the last few days I had grown less afraid of the ugly hole in my hip. I had indeed almost forgotten that question which had hovered on my lips the first day the doctor had dressed my wound. This morning as I drained the hot, steaming coffee, why, I had actually felt happy. The good times in Paris had already begun to simmer pleasantly in my brain. The Stormy Petrel, her blue eyes laughing at me across our little table in the café!

He must have seen how my face changed for he added quickly: "You see, it is this way. If you went now you might not even die."

There was a long silence, and then I made myself say it—made myself say it, though I knew too well the answer.

"And if I didn't die?"

"You might have to have your leg amputated. That you would not like, *n'est ce-pas*, my little American?"

Amputated! I said it over and over to myself with the cowardly courage of one who is bound to be trapped by no future dismay.

When I reached the bed my face must have been very white, whiter than ever; for my old major, being prepared for his departure, shot a sharp glance at me from under the deep cliff of eyebrow before he lifted his head and glared about the ward.

"*Il est un brave petit gars, l'aviateur américain,*" he announced loudly, with a warlike lift of his grey moustaches. And motioning the stretcher-bearer to bring him closer he placed a scratchy kiss on each of my cheeks. I forgot the terrible word I had been trying to learn. I was prouder of that salute than I had been of my decoration. It was harder to earn. I have never heard again of my old major but I cannot forget one who made the bitterest of all fights with such sublime purpose that he did not even know it was a fight.

The events of that day were too much. That night I began to bleed violently. I had one hemorrhage after another.

"Orderly," I called, "I'm bleeding to death."

The orderly's face said, "That's good." The orderly said nothing. He was hurried and tired. Instead of taking time to get a doctor he wrapped me up so tight that I was in agony and left me. I knew that he was worn and sleepless. A few hours more or less of pain didn't matter much. So I decided not to disturb him again that night.

But about midnight I heard a gasp. To my old major's bed they had just brought a captain with a bullet through his lungs. He was sitting up now, gurgling and spitting blood over himself and over me, who could not move out of his way. Finally his head jerked down. I cried out for the orderly. He pulled a sheet over the body and left it to be taken out in the morning.

On the other side of me that night was a lieutenant who had been shot in the leg. When they brought him in that morning his skin was green, his face and hands were full of blood. "Don't let them touch me, don't let them touch me," he had screamed when first he saw me. All that night, every time he heard a step, he begged me piteously not to let them hurt him. When I could stir through my own misery I gave him my handkerchief so that he could wipe the blood from his lips. I gave him too my piece of muslin to keep the flies off his face. Before dawn he was breathing heavily. For the third time that night I called the orderly.

"I can't do anything for him," said he irritably.

"He's dying," said I.

"What more could he want then?" growled the orderly.

After the last long gasp I reached over and at the cost of terrific pain held down his eyelids so they would stay closed. His face grew cold under my hand. The orderly, coming back on his rounds, pulled the sheet up over the body.

A sheeted form on my right, a sheeted form on my left. The stillness of death, after violent life, rang in my ears. It made more intense and solemn the stillness of my own brain. All through the long dawn I lay awake with the thought of my future. How still the future looked, how quenched!

To lose my usefulness, to come back to crippled life, this was the thing that had been haunting me since I had first caught sight of that black box in my hip. The doctor's word of the afternoon had made it all too definite. It held me in a vice, that one word. Yet my mind refused the pictures it created. I would not look, I would not look. And all the time those silent forms on each side of me made more rigid the terror of my doomed living. At last how I envied them. If only I could lie, long and lumpy, under one of those white sheets!

But I went on living through ten more days of haunted imprisonment—ten more days tortured for sleep that would not come, days when I was too heavy with weariness to brush the flies off my face, too hot to cover it with the muslin cloth; ten more nights more tortured than the day, nights dingy and endless and noisy with dying. Every night eight or twelve men found the easier way. Every morning stretcher-boxes came to carry out the dead. Every morning stretcher-bearers came to fill their places with the living. Not for five minutes did I ever see a bed vacant. Was it any wonder that in the hospital at V—— I lost all sense of the dignity of death? It had become a commonplace mechanism.

In a place where men died like flies, where there weren't half enough doctors or orderlies, the filth

of course was indescribable. Although the floors
were scrubbed every day, this cleansing could not
prevail against the constant stream of wounded.
As for the patients, they never had a drop of water on their bodies except when they were allowed
to wash hands and face every other morning. If
it had not been for the huge bottle of eau de Co-
logne with which the boys from the squad satu-
rated me, I think I should have died of nausea.

As I have said, such conditions will never ex-
ist again. The Verdun attack had overtaken
France without proper hospital equipment. I
never blamed those who worked here. On the contrary I have the highest respect for efforts which
were simply titanic. Every man wounded at Verdun passed through that hospital. Doctors, working day and night, often twelve hours at a stretch,
operated on one man after another as fast as they
could. Give a man the best you can, as fast as
you can; if he dies, let him die; if he lives, ship
him away where he can get better care; this was
the purpose of the place. And doctors and orderlies carried it out with superhuman heroism. If
at times their treatment of patients seemed appalling, the strain on them was more appalling.

The Verdun siege was taxing the Paris hospitals too. I heard rumours of how my blue-eyed

nurse was working. I had just one message from her. And I knew that no matter how crowded the hospital was, there would be a bed for me. Foster, who brought me her message, would not be down to see me again; he was off on an important mission. So during this time my chief comforts were Madame and the boys from the squad. Every afternoon some of the fellows came to see me, a sacrifice which I can never have a chance to repay. All of the boys but one who flew with me are dead now. I am sure that in their life of hard service there was no conflict more exacting than the day-by-day visit to this loathsome hospital.

As for Madame, I came to long more and more for the sight of that stiff white skirt, that separate look and crooning "*Mon fils.*" I stayed so long that the separate look became just a little more of a gift to me than to others. I was the oldest patient in point of time, the youngest in point of years. She treated me like a son. Every now and then she would snatch a moment to chat with me. It was in one of these moments that I opened up my heart to her on the subject of that dark fear which lately had begun to stalk me. I repeated to her my conversation with the doctor.

"Do you think," I asked, "that I shall lose this leg?"

How it comforted me to see her laugh away the suggestion! That was exactly what I wanted.

"You're sure there's no danger?" said I.

"Absolutely no," said she. "He's a clever fellow, that doctor. If you stay with him, he'll bring you through."

After that I was radiantly happy. If I could just see the nurse in Paris and then go back to my job! If only my fight up there in the air and my other one against weakness and thirst were not in vain, I could stand the filth and heat and pain.

And then came the change which made all my previous sufferings seem as naught. The skin on my hips had broken and festered. July heat and the solutions that were used kept my bed perpetually wet. For days I would lie without moving an inch in a reeking mass of blood, pus and perspiration. Only when my temperature went so many degrees above normal would my dressings be changed. This was usually about every fourth day. Then as I was lifted up for the trip to the dressing-table the hole in the bed made by my body would be black with blood and matter. In the hospitals of to-day, with their marvellous distribution of nurses and supplies, such a condition would be a disgrace. Then it could not be helped.

I was also getting such cramps that I asked the doctor if he couldn't straighten my leg.

"I've been going to tell you, my child," he said hesitatingly, "that I was afraid you'd have to have another operation."

"Hurrah!" I shouted. "Bully for you, Doc! That's the best news I've heard since we licked the crown prince!"

"My dear boy, are you"—he felt for the American slang he loved—"becoming nut-like?"

"No," I answered with a grin, "but I should go nutty soon if something didn't happen. I need a change, Doc. Anything would be better than this. Let's have that little 'op' right away before you forget it!"

"You're a good subject," laughed the doctor, getting me on the table without more ceremony. "This time I shall not even have to strap your hands. Now just wait a second till I open up this fellow over here."

He had exactly the air of a grocer saying to a friend, "One moment, till I cut off some cheese for this customer."

From my own table I watched the other operation. When the doctor finally turned back to me, his apron red and dripping as always, the man was gasping.

"He's gone," said the surgeon cheerfully, with no thought that his casual air might not prove bracing to me. Indeed it did not trouble me. I was, however, somewhat disturbed by the sunny opulence with which the orderly, listening to talk near him, was pouring chloroform on my mask.

"Make him give it to me easier, Doc," I begged.

Brushing him away, the doctor finished giving me the drug. I thrilled off into a flight more intoxicating than anything I had ever known.

The ecstasy was short. My sciatic nerve had been partly severed by one portion of the bullet. Now when my leg was stretched out for the first time, all the strands of the main nerve, which is as big as a finger, snapped off.

An explosive bullet in my hip, that bleeding journey through the barbed wire, probings, dressings, thirst, bedsores, cramp—these were mere discomforts compared to the agony that dragged me now from under the sheltering oblivion of ether after this operation.

"*Qu'est ce que c'est muth-muth?*" asked an aviator in the bed next mine. In a strangled way I had been crying for my mother.

Once that night I started up from a deep-drugged sleep with the sense of some one looking at me. It was my doctor. He was breathing fast and his hair was tousled. He had evidently hur-ried from somewhere to my bedside. The anxiety in his face arrested me.

"Shall I be all right, Doc? Shall I be as good as new?"

"I hope so, my little one; I hope so."

His look, his tone, his eyes which slid away from mine—these told me mercilessly what he would not say. The dimly lighted ward turned black, so black that I did not see him leave. My heart went down, down through endless sick distances. I knew now what I was coming back to.

Before this, except for those few horrible days when I had feared amputation, my long fight had meant to me only these tortured weeks in bed. After that I was to go back, young and vigorous, to my old job. When, up there in the air, I had chosen the middle road between a glorious living or more glorious dying, I had not thought of its leading elsewhere. Youth was the talisman I had taken with me on that journey. Twenty! What could happen to twenty except a stern, brief bout with pain from which youth would emerge victorious, but youthful still—twenty crowned by conflict!

Ah, and what really lay before me on the middle road? Age in youth. I might spend the rest of my life in a wheeled chair. Perhaps I might watch the boys flying, I who had meant to fly so far, I who should never fly again.

Why had I fought death there in the air, why had I gone through these hideous days, pitting my will against weakness and thirst? Was it for this, to be lame, crippled, a burden for the rest of my existence?

My mental pain, as violent as that of my tortured body, lasted all through the day and night. Then in the agonised days that followed nothing was left of me but tormented flesh. My mind was in a stupor. My will was dead. I was not even groping. No longer an active force, my brain became only a listless page upon which were written haphazard bits of memory and thought.

A sick man's thoughts are often like that. And I was sick now, sick in body and spirit as I had never been before. In those moments, half conscious, half drugged, it isn't the big things of life that come back. It's the song, the almost forgotten verse that haunts. So now in me, among the mouse-like, scampering thoughts, gnawed always one fragment of poetry:

"My life has crept so long on a broken wing."

This line, read I know not where or when, buried under years of forgetfulness, came and went and came again until I thought I should go mad.

Yes, day after day my life had crept, day upon day it was creeping. My fingers were spread on the coverlet, as bleached and bony as a spray of coral. Laying my right hand over my left, I slid the under one out and put it on top. I piled one hand on the other till I could reach no higher. That had become my life. Each day it slid from under at night. Morning lifted it to the top of another. It was like the wool my mother used to card, one carding stacked upon another until the pile, soft and thick, grew too tall for childish eyes to follow. My days had thickened; their pile was growing tall.

My mother, ah, my mother! She who had always been to me a battle-cry, she whose name I had flung to the drowning air when I had made my fight for life there above the clouds! Why was it now that the memory of her could no longer bring back my courage? When I crept home on crutches she would be waiting for me on the porch as she used to wait when I came home from school, her apron snowy as her hair, the smell of hot biscuits following through the open door, on her dear, dark face love, love ineffable. My broken wing would make no difference to her; I should be dearer to her now than ever before. Yet as I saw myself in her eyes, saw her pity coming forever between me and a changed world, I realised more heartbreakingly just what that changed world would be. That now she must always be making it up to me—scalding tears for her and for myself broke through my prisoned mind.

"My life has crept so long on a broken wing."

—Again the scampering thoughts after that gnawing refrain.

Once I shot an old stray tom in our back yard. He kicked, then tumbled over and over before he began creeping. It was my first shot and I fired again to put him out of his misery. I never could forget his face as he looked at me. He didn't think I'd do it. That's the way men kick and curl up into shavings, then creep off on a broken wing.

What was that? Through the open windows of the ward, across the surf of surging guns, fell splashes of music. A band was playing "Sympathy." Just two years ago at the Texas fort I had danced with Jasmine on those waves of melody. She had, I remembered, a soft allure in her eyes.

So had the girl that used to give me bread from the New Orleans bakery. So had the girl that used to take my order in the Paris cabby's café.

Always, everywhere, I had met eyes that softened alluringly. Should I ever meet them again? Should I ever dance again? Never dance again! I had not thought of that. I looked down the row of beds and my eyes widened with the full terror of what I had lost.

"My life has crept so long on a broken wing."

Yes, I should go creeping to Paris but not to those gay little dinners where the nurse with the blue eyes would laugh at me across our corner table. Through these pestilent weeks there had been one invigorating thought. When my longing for her would become as intolerable as my thirst had been, I would close my eyes and summon her. In a moment I could forget the rows of cots with their human fragments, the gasps of dying men, the curses of those who must live, even my own increasing pain. For the miracle of her presence was upon me. The tonic laugh, the tender, enfolding glance, the moment when I would first make her believe my love, the moment when she would let me know hers—in the very hope of these lay healing.

But now! There would be no more promise in her eyes, only pity. She would be taking me out, not I her; she would be taking me to the Bois in a wheeled chair. She would protect me as she had the crippled soldier in the Dublin station. Stuffing my pillow in my mouth so that no one would hear me, I cried as I had never cried in my whole life.

Pity! That was all there was left for me in this world. Her pity! *That* I could not bear. My brain, which had so long seemed a mere listless page, was at last beginning to write—write its defiance to a world of pitying eyes.

In one blinding second I knew what I wanted. It was death. Twice before it had seemed the easiest way. Now it was the only way. Now everything in me cried out for death—death the prize to be wrested from mocking Life. With rage in my heart at life, I made up my mind to die.

Each anguished day I was growing weaker. Each anguished day I was drawing nearer that radiant goal where the I should cease to be. At last it came, the sure moment. Peace, deep and immense, descended upon me. I was falling softly, smoothly into death.

"He's dying," said a French soldier who had been calling with a friend upon my neighbour.

"Yes," responded the other as they started for the door. Then pausing by my bed he added, "He has fought long, the little American, but now *helas!* he has lost the will to fight."

Lost the will to fight! The low, quick voice, the pitying disposal of me—how was it that these pierced my twilit soul; that they reached some strata of obstinacy which nothing else, not even my mother, had been able to touch? In a second I saw myself for what I was, a pitiable coward, giving up life because it was no longer easy. Now, if ever, the world needed men, needed every atom of usefulness, however curtailed, to carry on the battle against slavery. Yet because I could not be useful in the way I wanted——

Another undertow of drugged pain, of drugging weakness. The light behind me was growing dimmer. Life now seemed like the lamp in the window of the cottage we are leaving. I had a moment's heartbreaking desolation at the thought of that leaving. The lamp in the window, the cosy warmth that I had known so well—home, life! Yet over there on the far bank the other lights called me. Only one moment's terror of leaving, only one moment's yielding to that swift undertow, and the unknown lights would be mine. I was going; yes, I was going. The near shore, the light in the window, slipping. Unless—my God! There was only a second's time! And then——

Even now I wonder how I did it, how against the vision of those far lights before me I pulled my will from every remote, imprisoned part of me.

"Jacques," I whispered to the aviator next me. He turned his head.

"Jacques—quick! I'm dying." By a giant effort I moved my eyes toward his. "When I go to sleep, wake me! Don't let me——"

Utterly exhausted I closed my eyes again.

"*Reveillez-vous! Reveillez-vous!*"

Jacques's voice called me back from the far lights.

"Oh—yes!" I made myself answer.

Only for one second. Then once more I felt myself going.

"*Reveillez-vous! Reveillez-vous!*"

"Oh—yes!"

So over and over again we fought together, the wounded aviator and I. For four hours he kept me alive. Then at six o'clock I said weakly: "It's all right, Jacques. I'm not going to die."

I had made my third fight. I had come back to stay.

In the days and weeks that followed I had many black moods. There were longs hours when that haunting line of verse "My life has crept so long on a broken wing" sounded like doom itself. Then it was I wondered why I had come back to my hampered life, why I had not listened to those lights that called me from afar? What did the future hold for me, I wondered bitterly, what use could I ever be again, I and my broken wing?

Gradually, however, something was growing up in me. Very faint and dim at first, it reached feebly through the dark mists. Then, no longer groping, it thrust out strong and free, and at last I knew why I had stayed.

Life is like that always, I think. First comes the obstinate impulse. One does a thing instinctively, without any thought. It is not until long afterward that one sees clearly the purpose of that impulse. That is why my whole philosophy tarried so late after my supreme instinct not to be a quitter.

What helped me most to this vision was the remembrance of those crippled men I had seen in Ireland as I passed through on my way to France.

They had been fitted with artificial arms and legs
and the one expression on each face had touched
me then in the midst of my confident youth. Now
it came back to me again, that one repeated look,
and as I lay here I knew that my own face was
coming to wear the same expression. It was that
of radiant gratitude for to-day.

Gratitude for to-day! How few before this
war knew anything about that peace, how little I
myself had comprehended it until these last few
days! Up to this time I had been one of a world
of little men, all wondering what they should be
doing at thirty, fearing that they would not have
enough by forty, dogged forever and forever by
an implacable to-morrow. That is what I should
always have been had not the explosive bullet
begun my real fight. Now I was healed forever
of fear. Life could no longer terrify me with to-
morrow—me who had been through the worst.
From this time forth I should live each day as it
came.

But there was more than this. So long as a
man is haunted by what to-morrow can do to him,
so long as his life is made up of fearful limita-
tions, he is always on the outside of the world.
I myself, flying for France, aware of the noble
righteousness of her cause, was nevertheless mere-

ly conferring. Not until I lay here stricken for France was I really absorbed by that cause. France, the Allies, Freedom—now at last I was part of the world. Freed of all shrewd little personal calculations, freed forever from fear of what would happen to me, I saw that nothing mattered but the common cause. Lying here in this terrible hospital, I on my broken wing was permitted a vision of the world as a whole which the untouched can never know. Nothing can ever take it away from me. It is life's high gift to the severely wounded.

And after accepting the worst, the worst passed me by.

Still under the delusion that his peculiar skill alone could save me, the doctor, who was finally ordered to Paris, said he would ship me on to the Appleton Hospital, where he would join me in a few days.

"And remember," said he, "tell the physician there that I understand your case and that no one is to touch you till I have you transferred to my own hospital."

So unexpectedly, so accidentally came the release I had waited for. No more filth, no more loneliness, no more horror. I burst into tears.

The morning procession had begun. Stretcher-boxes were carrying out the night's harvest of the dead. In a moment all beds would be filled again, mine and those in which these sheeted forms had lain. At the doorway the line was halted by Madame who embraced me in farewell.

"*Adieu, petit américain!*" came a chorus of cries from the ward.

I looked back at the whitewashed walls within which I had found a talisman stronger, surer, more enduring than the talisman of youth.

"*Adieu, adieu, adieu!*" I cried brokenly to my gallant comrades of the middle road.

The doctor followed my stretcher to the ambulance.

"It will be a hard ride," he said in a low voice. "Other doctors, not knowing your condition, may not give it to you. I trust you." He pressed into my hand a pellet of morphine.

It was a hard ride. The swinging of the hospital train hurt unbearably. By this time I was practically a drug fiend; like gold I hoarded my little fund of forgetfulness. But in the night I could endure no more.

"I'll never need it worse than now," I decided.

Hardly had I swallowed the pellet when the train doctor for the first time that night bent over my berth.

"Suffering much?" he asked.

"Yes," said I.

I was surprised when he took out his needle. Should I tell him? No. I could not get too much.

"Go ahead, Doc," I said.

He jabbed in the needle. In ten minutes I was asleep.

I awoke in Paris.

I awoke suffering and desolate. For weeks of agony I had thought of Paris as a refuge. I had vaguely expected the Gare la Chapelle to wipe away all pain. I had vaguely expected it to be filled with friends. As I lay now on my stretcher, waiting with a hundred others to be taken to the hospitals, I ached with the emptiness that follows expectation. I was one of many wounded. That was all. The stretcher-bearers were new. Every face that I saw was strange and uncaring. Foster, I knew, was out of town. But she—my lip quivered—she had not come to meet me. Was she away when my last message came? Did she receive it and not care? The blood beat up into my face; my ear-drums throbbed sickeningly.

A French woman in the station poured some coffee down my throat. Three drivers, all strangers to me, carried me to a car. How queer to go through Paris as a wounded man. Was it I, was it I? I kept looking out of the back window, trying to see where we were driving. We were going through the Bois to find the best roads—that much I could see.

Then we reached the receiving hospital. The old familiar spots, the old familiar faces, only increased my desolation. For no one knew me. Old friends—doctors, nurses, drivers—passed me by. They glanced at my stretcher, at my bleached, bony face, at my arms like matches—and went on. I tried to call out but was too weak.

"Bob!" By a terrific effort I made a driver hear me. "Bob, don't you know me? Byrd?"

"Oh, Byrd, by gee!" He hardly stopped to greet me. "Boys, take this stretcher to Miss Gale's office. She's been looking for you every day all summer. I'll let her know."

Ah, her face! I saw it through a glory that smote me, a peace that bore me up. Pain and heartache—I had never known them. There was only one fact now in all the world. That was her dear, blinding presence. Shutting my eyes to hide the tears, I tried to hold up my arms. I could not speak.

Kneeling there beside me in her little office, she held me close. Her tears were on my cheeks. My head slipped to her shoulder. For the first time in my life I had fainted—with joy.

CHAPTER VI

COMING out of that swoon, I knew with a sick man's sensibility one thing: the Stormy Petrel and the Swallow had flown. In their places were Miss Gale, a highly specialised surgical nurse, and her patient, Richard Byrd, a man sick unto death, living only through a strength of spirit that had grown from bodily anguish.

It was Miss Gale who spoke to me that first day as soon as I came out of the trance of joy. "And now," said she, "you must have a bath."

"Oh, let me go to bed," I begged from the stretcher where I still lay strapped to the board upon which the doctor at V—— had tied me for the journey. "A day or so more doesn't matter to a man who hasn't bathed for six weeks. I'm so tired!"

"Very well, you shall go to bed, then," she said.

A moment more and I was carried to a ward where nine other officers lay. I was given the bed by the window. I did not know until long afterwards how difficult it had been for my nurse through all the Verdun siege, to keep that bed for me.

Worn out with excitement, lulled by the white peace of the room and the secure sense of home, I dropped asleep. When I awoke Miss Gale and a man were bending over me. He was a powerful young fellow with shining black eyes and thick black hair that fell in rope-like ridges. I felt an instant dislike for him. Miss Gale introduced him as Olson, the ward physician.

"Sorry, doctor," I said, "but I promised my physician at V—— that no one should touch me till he came. He'll be here this afternoon."

My doctor had so impressed this upon me that I grew excited at the thought of disobeying him. Seeing my intensity, Miss Gale yielded.

"We might wait till his doctor comes, then," she suggested, and with a shrug Olson left.

But by late afternoon my pain had increased and the doctor had not come. I was still protesting, however, that I could have no other surgeon.

"I can't humour you any longer," said Miss Gale, with professional severity. "No one doctor is indispensable to any case and there is no reason for you to suffer any more than you can help."

She summoned Olson and when he came I made one last protest.

"If you take off the board, don't cut the dressings," I implored. "I promised my doctor."

"All right, I won't," said Olson.

At an exclamation I looked around. He had taken off the bandage!

"You promised you wouldn't cut the dressings," I said.

"Absolutely necessary, my dear fellow. Miss Gale, come here!"

She gave a little cry when she saw me.

As I have said, nothing but my face and hands had been washed while I was at V——. Now my skin had entirely changed. I was black. Next day they began the task of bathing me. For this purpose they used soft soap and gasoline. It was more than a month before I was entirely clean.

Because of the wearisome trip I had undergone, I was given that first night my usual amount of morphine. Still soothed by the sense of home-coming, still cherished by merry blue eyes that could soften to tears, I slept.

The next day my pain was intense. The bed-sores, too, which I had developed at V—— were frightful. For these the nurse tried an air mattress; but the heat of the rubber made the sores worse. Finally she got a special bed constructed for just such a case as mine.

The head surgeon was out of town and my doctor from V—— had not yet come, so I was still entirely under the care of Olson. He was a splendid specimen of American vigour. He had come to France only for adventure. He had not a care in the world, either for himself or any one else. He had never known what pain meant and he had not the imagination to conceive it. So when, that second night, I asked for my morphine, he refused it. I was by now practically a drug fiend. And to be cut off suddenly was appalling. So, swallowing my pride and my distaste for the man, I begged him to cut me off gradually.

"My dear fellow——" and seating himself beside my bed, the ward doctor gave me a long talk on the evils of morphine.

"Look here, Doc," I broke in at last, "you can't tell me anything about the horrors of dope. I'm a dope fiend. That's just the point. Now treat me like an intelligent man, not like a baby. I'm in ghastly pain. You know, and I know that the human structure can't stand everything. A man can die from brutal pain alone. Now I've lived on morphine straight for three weeks. If I asked you to keep up my allowance, that would be different. But I ask you just to cut me off gradually."

I sank back exhausted.

"It won't do," he said, with a patronising shake of his head. "Some day you'll thank me. I'll tell the night nurse to give you some aspirin."

Aspirin! How I hated him as he walked off! How I hated that glossy, ridge-like hair, the clear black and white of his eyes! I clenched my hands in weak, helpless fury. If I were cut off at once from any alleviating drug, I should die of pain. That I knew.

Then as I lay there I thought of those first days at V—— when every nerve in my body had been gnawed by the longing for water. But that hunger was as nothing compared to this. In the agony of my craving I forgot the agony of my body. My mother, my nurse—everything that was I—was lost in my abject longing for the thing to make me forget them all.

I closed my eyes. I tried to shut out the ravenous vision. But the closed lids only bound it more tightly. I and the longing, the longing and I— together we rode. And my heart grew so feeble that I thought I was dying.

Then suddenly like a flake a hand fell on my forehead. It didn't go away like a flake, however. It just stayed and cooled me and kept drawing out of me my fevered longing. Ah, my nurse! That was what her hand always did to me. It was not like the touch of Jasmine, pressing in her ruthless glamour, making you conscious every minute that she was she. Instead, it kept drawing out from you all unloveliness.

I was thinking that when I opened my eyes. And then as I looked at her it all came back. I was beaten by wave after wave of savage hunger. At that moment there was nothing I would not have done to get morphine.

As I lay there looking at her it came back to me—the sick man's craft which had once made me think that if I could only *look* as thirsty as I was, Dover Manley would get me something to drink.

What if she were a nurse? What if it were against the regulations?

"I shan't see you again until to-morrow. Is there anything you want before I go?"

The cool silver kindness of her voice fell across my abject craving. At that moment I hated her goodness, hated that tone in her voice that always expected the best of you. If she had ever seemed once on her guard against the worst in you—I clenched my hands in helpless fury. No, I could not ask my nurse to get me morphine.

But as I saw her white figure drift through the evening dimness of the ward my resolve to get what I wanted was just as violent as ever. Ignobly I began to run over all the people I had known in Paris. Foster? Out of town. Besides he wasn't that kind. Neither were any of my other old friends that kind. But who, who? Surely there must be somebody, some mere acquaintance, perhaps, some kindly, unscrupulous soul that would help a poor slave to more of his slavery.

And then all of a sudden it came to me—the memory of the little cocotte whose gloves I had appropriated. I had smiled, half in amusement, half in embarrassment, when she had said, "If you ever need a friend." But on that memorable night of my first dinner with my nurse when I had returned the gloves to the little girl, she had prevailed upon me to take her address. Ah, yes, thank fortune, I had it. The mere fact of writing it—the glamour of the evening—something—had impressed it upon my mind. She was Mademoiselle Marpas. She lived on the Rue Valette, near the Pantheon. Hardly able to conceal my eagerness, I called the night nurse. I directed her to send to the Rue Valette and beg Mademoiselle Marpas to visit me next day. The nurse raised her eyebrows a little. What did I care what she was thinking? To-morrow, yes, to-morrow, I should have my drug. And through the long torture of the night I lay, hoping she would come to me, fearing lest she might have moved away.

Early the next morning in she walked, my little cocotte. With her short skirt and her gay little hat tilted over her long, narrow blue eyes, she was like a saucy paroket. A little ripple went over the ward. It was not unusual for parokets to visit the ward, but this was an extremely saucy one. And as she was conducted to my bed, her voice carried to every corner of the room.

"*Mais, non.* There is some mistake. I never saw you before, *monsieur.*"

It was even more embarrassing than that night at the café when I had returned her gloves. But with my eye on the door where I dreaded every moment to see the figure of my nurse, I managed to recall to her our former meetings. She remembered then and once again she was covering my hand with kisses. "Oh, *mon pauvre, mon pauvre,*" she kept saying over and over again, in that crinkly, croony way that Madame at V—— had, that every French woman's voice falls into so magically.

I interrupted her. "Morphine," I whispered, "I must have it. Do you know any place where you could get it for me?"

She nodded her head. She kissed my hands. And as she left me another ripple went over the ward. It was just ending when my nurse entered the room.

She had not recognised the saucy little girl. She had not even known that she was visiting me. I actually gloated over the realisation of it as I watched her approach my bed.

No, she did not know that morning. But in the afternoon, as luck would have it, Mlle. Marpas came in with my pellets just as the nurse was leaving. The two women stared at each other and I stared at them both.

"This is—old friend of mine, Miss Gale," I muttered in confusion. "Gloves—I took hers, remember I told you?"

Quite evidently Miss Gale did remember. The memory of that night at the restaurant was gathering in the blue eyes even before I spoke. Yet the incident of the gloves did not explain just exactly why Mlle. Marpas happened to be here this instant nor why through all this interlude of pain I had managed to keep in touch with her. I saw bewilderment—perhaps even a moment's hurt—cross her face.

I saw them—ah, yes, but all in a furious sudden I did not care. All I cared for was those three milky pellets in the little cocotte's hand. And as I stared into the long narrow blue eyes of Mlle. Marpas I was blind and stiff and sick with the thought of the releasing joy now so tantalisingly near, so tantalisingly delayed. Oh, when would my nurse go? When would she leave me alone with the drug for which I had waited all that long night? Careless now of what Miss Gale would think, I fixed upon her one look of dumb, ruthless misery.

She met the look and the little hurt in her eyes deepened. Bah! What did I care? And when at last she turned her back upon us I grabbed the cocotte's hand.

"Quick, for God's sake," I whispered, "I'm going crazy."

It was about two hours after that when Miss Gale again returned to my bedside. By this time every nerve of my body had been smoothed down. I looked at my nurse in a kind of rosy compunction. Oh, how good she was, how much better than any one else in this world! As I chatted with her I became wildly joyous.

When she first came up to me there may have been still on her face a little of the proud hurt with which she had left me. But as I grew more and more talkative, as she heard my gay jokes, her look slowly changed. Quite suddenly she picked up my hand and took my pulse.

She suspected me. No, she knew. Even now on the full tide of my drug, I was aghast. For I realised that it would be her duty as a nurse to report me to Dr. Olson. And as I looked at the silent white figure, as I felt my blood flow up to those cool white fingers—flow and ebb away—every atom of my self-respect disappeared. More than that. I lost the man's wish to look well in his beloved's eyes. But in that one long, beseeching look which I did give to her I laid bare all of my weakness.

Without a word she turned away from me. And when several minutes later Dr. Olson came over to my bed my heart went down at what I knew he was about to say.

"Well, Byrd," he commenced and his hard red cheeks wagged in triumph.

I was too miserable to speak and I could hardly believe it when, taking my pulse, he announced complacently, "Doing fine, old man. Eyes much brighter. Pulse better. See what I told you, huh? Why, you'd have been a regular drug-fiend if you hadn't met up with me."

Oh, how good she was, how much better than any one else in the world! As Olson left me for

the night, as I took one of the magic pellets which
Mlle. Marpas had left me, I blessed the pity that
could transcend all sense of duty. My nurse had
known, yet she had not told.

The little cocotte came the next day with more
morphine. This time I diminished the doses. The
next time she brought me some pellets I reduced
them still more. And by the end of two weeks I
was able to get along with only the bromides
which the night nurse gave me.

In the meantime the doctor from V—— had finally come. He was many days later than his
schedule and Miss Gale had refused to allow me
to keep that old promise to him. It was indeed
fortunate. Had I waited for his attention I
should soon have been beyond the need of it. I
had been long enough the victim of his kindly egotism, of a judgment that had placed his knowledge of my case against care, sanitation and science. Had he only shipped me to Paris when I
was first wounded I should have been spared
much. As it was, I reached there just in time.
Just in time I came to my nurse.

It was one morning just after I had broken off
the morphine habit that Miss Gale first brought
to me the surgeon who was to bring me finally
from my twilight world. He was a big man, grey

and grave and steady; and no familiarity with suffering could ever make him careless of it. Now as he looked down at me there was such a quick, sweet touching of his spirit that I loved him from that moment. And I can never say enough of this man whose kindliness came from real seeing and who was as shocked by a sight of my suffering as he must have been at that of the first wounded man he ever saw.

As he examined my wound, there was none of the shallow cheeriness of the doctor at V——. Tenderly as he could he told me the truth.

"You're in a pretty bad way, my boy," said he, "but I think I know what you need and I'm going to try to make you glad to be alive once more."

I looked from his face to that of my nurse.

"Do you think in time—not right now, of course—but later on—oh, doctor, do you think I can walk on crutches?"

Sharply my nurse turned aside her head; and when she turned it back to me I could see that her lashes were wet. Ah, her pity, her wonderful pity! How it followed me through everything, how it seemed to make more radiant now the answer of my doctor!

"My dear boy," said he, "I can't promise any-

thing. But I'm going to try to get you out of this
bed."

God! What a journey was before me! It
was well I did not know. First of all, the head
surgeon put me in an extension. As the ball and
socket in my hip had been shot away this process
was necessary to prevent my leg from becoming
any shorter than it already was.

The extension was extremely painful. That
you may understand why this was so, let me explain. Over a pulley was a cord with leaden
weights which were attached to my leg by strips
of canvas glued to the skin. These weights, which
made continual tension on my leg, were increased
by half a pound a day until twenty pounds were
reached. Thus the muscles, instead of contracting as they had at V——, were held taut and the
bone was allowed to grow.

The stretching of the muscles meant an inces-
sant ache; the glue kept my flesh itching; the
nerves, shut off from any air, burned until my leg
seemed a red-hot iron. As I've said before, my
sciatic nerve had snapped; and it was because of
this fact that I now developed foot-drop and had
to have a five-pound weight attached to my foot.
Meanwhile the bedsores I had developed at V——

became so painful that I had to lie on a rubber ring. At the height of my misery I had an abscess in my ear. And at the height of the abcess I got the mumps!

The grotesque malady of childhood seemed to rob my suffering of all dignity. To see in a mirror my skeleton-like face swollen into bags, to have what little food I could take poured down my throat—these ludicrous details overcame me more thoroughly than all the severe suffering that had gone before them. During the ten days that I was mump-bound, I lost for the moment all the uplift of those last days at V——. I was in fact as peevish as a six-year-old. The only thing I wanted was my nurse. And when she could not be with me I sulked all the time. She oughtn't to neglect me like this, I thought. It was unjust, it was cruel.

One morning as I lay there with hot applications on those foolish pouches I watched her coming through the ward. She never glanced in my direction. She was busy looking at each man's dressings. I saw the look that a young Frenchman was giving her. There was the same impatient wanting of her on his face that there must have been on my own. And for the first time I realised that Miss Gale was not *my* nurse. She was the young Frenchman's there—she was everybody's. And with a sudden aching emptiness I realised I had been measuring Miss Gale's interest in me by my own interest in her. I recalled now the tears with which she had met me—how, unconsciously, against my clearer vision, I had been treasuring them.

She was now at the bed next to mine. A middle-aged *chasseur* who had lost both his arms was lying here. As she turned back the covers to look at his dressings, something in the whole gesture of her body stabbed me with a sense of her remoteness. Heavens, how free her mind was of me, of me whose only thought was of her! There is nothing comparable to the loneliness of one who has been imagining closeness; and what I felt now was even more desperate than the hurt which, when I was the Swallow and she was the Stormy Petrel, she had given me that morning as, tingling with memories of her at our first little dinner, I had come in from camp to find her absorbed in charts and business.

She felt the *chasseur's* bandages. The whiff of his antiseptics will always be joined sickeningly with my memory of that moment. Then I heard her speak to the ward physician.

"Don't you think, doctor, that these bandages are just a little too tight?"

Ah, yes, I thought bitterly, she would miss no detail. She was a nurse, not a woman. And the life of a nurse—a good nurse, that is—is one of passionate routine. She must care for the suffering, not for the sufferer.

At last she came over to my bed. With what was left of my face from the mumps I looked up at her indignantly, reproachfully.

Her own face broke up into little nooks and crannies. For the first time I resented them.

"Thpoth I'm funny 'nough," I managed to articulate. Mumps and dignity were, I found, difficult to maintain at the same time.

In an instant the nooks and crannies disappeared. "Oh, my poor boy," she whispered. "It just seems the last straw, doesn't it?" Then again her face and tone changed. "Do you know when I had the mumps?" she said. "Why, it was on Christmas Day and I was just six years old. Fancy what that means! Nothing good to eat—swallowing a few spoonfuls of broth when the rest are eating turkey and mince-pie. I always look back on that as one of the tragedies of my life."

"I dare say it was the only tragedy." That was what I might have said had not the beastly mumps interfered with the conversational service. As it was, I looked at her more resentfully than ever. I had the feeling that she was talking to me, was humouring me with conversation, just as if she were a grown-up person trying to make some sick child forget his illness.

She did not seem to notice how I was looking at her. "Never mind," said she as she began to examine my dressings, "the mumps will soon be over, you know. And when you're well of them— just guess what we're going to have."

"What?" I murmured with fretful bitterness.

"Why, sweetbreads and mushrooms—all sorts of good things. A lot of your old friends among the ambulance corps have been wanting to know what they could do for you and I told them they were to buy you something good to eat. Then we'll see. 'I am the cook and the captain bold and the nurse of the Nancy Brig,' " she quoted merrily as she touched my bandages.

"Oh, don't take any bother for me," I retorted with rancorous emphasis on the last word.

At my words her face broke up again into the objectionable nooks and crannies. And when she left me that morning I felt that she had seen through all my ungraciousness and was a little bit amused by it.

That little scene was only the prelude of many more phases of suffering. First of all an abscess caused by the explosive bullet formed in my abdomen. The pain from this was intense; and it was only an operation which relieved the terrible pressure.

Meanwhile my wound was as torturing as ever. Twice a day Olson dressed it and at each dressing, involving as it did contact with the sciatic nerve, I stuffed my handkerchief into my mouth and covered my head with the pillow so that I might scream unheard. During this time, of course, I took no morphine. And, too nervous to sleep at night, I got only a few snatches by day. For one month I never missed the quarter hour struck all night on a nearby clock.

It was due to the Carrel system of irrigation, which has saved so many lives during the war, that my wound did gradually begin to heal. Although they have heard of it vaguely, many people do not know just what this great healing irrigation means. It is for their benefit that I explain. The Carrel system consists of a bulb to which is attached a main tube and various smaller tubes. The bulb is filled with a solution which every two hours is flushed through the tubes. In this way the whole body is sprayed as by a garden hose.

But although this treatment helped my wound, the acid in its solution irritated the bedsores. In spite of all the 'care I was receiving, they grew worse and worse. There were nights when I could not let my back touch the bed, when I lay on my hands until they cramped. Also other abscesses developed. Each of these had to be operated upon. And four times I was carried to the "billiard table," as was popularly known the operating table. I never minded these incisions. The fact of the matter was that, cut off from morphine as I now was, the anæsthetic was the one refuge from pain, the one escape to rosy peace.

Along with the Carrel system were kept up the suspension weights on my leg. At last these were removed to give way to a plaster cast in which I lived for many months. Now from chest to knee I was rolled in plaster which, though not much thicker than an eggshell, was as hard as iron. Windows were made in the cast for my bed-sores, which at last began to improve. Windows were made, too, so that my wound might be dressed. Save for these my shell was implacable.

Yet in spite of all I endured, the year and a half in this hospital passed more quickly than six weeks at V——. Radiant cleanliness, the luxury of baths and of snowy linen, smokes to soothe my hours of pain, above all the trained and sympathetic care of women after the hurried attention of those poor driven orderlies at V——, the deft science which has helped so many to come back from the middle road—these were the miracles of the Appleton Hospital.

Meanwhile what of the vision which I have called life's high gift to the severely wounded? It did not always burn steadily ahead of me. That was too much to expect. There were days when, pulled down by bitter undertows of pain, I longed again for death. There were days when the vision flickered dimly. Yet it was there. I could always come back to it. Each time that I came back I felt more sure of it.

Strangely enough, the one person who had hindered the steadiness of this vision was the one person I might have expected to keep it before me. That was my nurse. When I first came to this hospital, I had thought I was healed of the future, of all little plans for to-morrow. But from the moment her tears fell on my face there in her office, I had been unconseiously counting on those tears. Forgetting that I had learned to live in to-day, I began wanting Eileen Gale for my to-morrow. I wanted her to want me. I wanted her—sealed—sure—my own forever.

Of course I never put that feeling into even my mind's words. I think I should have been horrified if any one had suggested that I, Richard Byrd, a man cut off from youth and normal youthful avenues, could be mean enough to ask such love. And it was only that day when I was so ignobly stung by her attention to the *chasseur* in the bed next to mine, when I saw how independent was her mind of any longing for me, how cruelly wide was her pity—only that day did I realise what I had been wanting.

I have told you how that day I felt a kind of morose loneliness. In my sickness, I had even shown her my bitterness that she could think of others when I thought only of her. For weeks I forgot that freeing vision of my days at V——. I was bound once again by the longing to make sure of my to-morrow.

It was, after all, the first real test of my philosophy. Bodily adventure, haphazard romance of eyes that looked into mine with soft allure, dancing—these had all called to me and I had been able to silence their voices. Yet I was far from them when I gave them up. Now—Eileen Gale —she was not far. She was near me every day— near, yet not close. I could never make her close. I had not the right.

For days, through all my physical suffering, there was this terrible protest of spirit. Here was I twenty-two and—powerless. By every right of youth she should be mine. Yet here I lay—I and my broken wing—my youth denied, myself the poor maimed thing which took its place in her eyes only because it was one of the hundreds of others that needed her care.

It must have been weeks that I suffered this torment. Longing to see her, miserable when she was away from me, I was even more tortured when she was actually with me. Sometimes, indeed, my protest broke into desperate hope. I treasured every little sign. I tried to read into some word or gesture a tenderness that was for me, Richard Byrd, and not for the mere broken wing. I even went back to that time when the little cocotte brought me my morphine. Miss Gale had not understood. Plainly for one minute she had been hurt. That had been nothing to me at the moment. Then I had wanted only one thing—my drug. Now, however—hurt, hurt, hurt! I almost shouted the word to myself. Buffeted by physical pain in almost every part of me, I could yet cling to this memory. That look was not like the tears with which she had met me—tears which she might have given to any poor boy

she had once known full of health and merriment.
It was a tribute to me, the man. It showed me
what I might have become to her if Life had not
chosen to rob me.

Yet, always catching myself in time, I sternly
put away the thought of Eileen Gale in any rela-
tion save that of the friendly nurse who liked me
better than her other patients only because she
happened to know me a little, because she had
once sat opposite to me at a snowy table from
which Christmas poinsettias broke into bloom. So
the days went by until that one morning when
Eileen Gale did not come to me at seven with the
breakfast which she herself often prepared.

"Where's—where's Miss Gale?" I stammered
to Miss Sally May, the little Baltimore nurse.

"Grippe," answered Miss Sally. "They're
afraid she's getting pneumonia."

I stared at her incredulously. She—sick? I
somehow could not believe it. Why—why she
was a nurse. It was her business to be well, to
be here taking care of me. And then after the
little Baltimore nurse had gone I realised as I
took a mechanical sip of coffee how much I had
always taken Eileen Gale for granted—taken her
for granted and—wanted her.

There were ten terrible days ahead. During

this time Dr. Olson operated on the first of my abscesses. This relieved the pressure on my body
which had dragged me to and fro as if I were
bound to the back of some frantic wild beast. The
comparative freedom from pain left me more free
to miss Eileen Gale, to ache for the sight of her
coming through the door of the ward, for the
touch of her cool, firm fingers, for the merry laugh
that always seemed to be folding in and out.

She had not got pneumonia. After one day of
dread I found out that I had really nothing to
fear for her. All I went through now was the
aching emptiness of these hours away from her. I
was homesick as I had never been in my life.

One morning I was watching Miss Sally May
looking at the bandages of the wounded *chasseur*
on my right. At the first whiff of the antiseptics,
it all came back to me—just how Eileen had
looked that morning when I had resented her un-
distracted care of him. And like a wave it broke
over me—my new seeing.

"Oh," I found myself thinking passionately, "if
I could only see you—here—at his side—right
now! Taking care of him, taking care of me—
what does it matter which—just so long as I can
see you."

That was the way I learned my new lesson—

the lesson that was really part of my old one. I knew now that I had been wanting Eileen Gale to give, not to be. I saw that it was just because she always would be strong enough and separate enough to follow her duty in the face of any op-posing personal inclination, that I loved her so much. I had wanted her for mine. Yet always mine she would be. For it is only the soul which really understands and loves another soul, that truly possesses. I needed no other seal, no sign for the morrow. And to-day that gave me a sight of her, that gave me even a thought of her—who, even the meanest, could ask for more than that?

So the vision that had come to me at V—— was at last made perfect by my love for Eileen Gale. There were times when I slipped again into dark-ness, when I longed for death to put an end to the mocking wish that she might be mine in the old human way. But these times were few and more and more I was content with the day's bless-ing of her presence.

*   *   *

The long night had trudged heavily away. The last hour, with a furtive glance over its shoulder at the coming dawn, hurried its steps. In that kind darkness before morning, my tightened nerves relaxed. My lids, heavy with sleeplessness, dropped, lifted again to the cosy dusk of the ward, dropped once more and shut me in to bliss. . . .

I was back in El Paso. I was starting down to the bakery. Some one followed me out to the front lawn—was it mother, was it a girl? I could never tell; but always it was a woman's presence. She bent over the crocus bed under the magnolias. "They're pushing on their little toes, trying to get their heads up through the ground," she said. I kissed the back of the bent neck and swung off down the street in glorious strides. Beside this intoxication motion, flying was dull. To walk, to work—here was adventure! . . .

My eyes, opened slowly by the daylight, fell on the tree-tops outside my window. It was the same dream, the dream of walking, drunk with my own vigour, that I had had for months every morning at this hour. And always my disillusioned eyes had opened not on the magnolias of El Paso but on the poplars outside the Appleton Ambulance in Paris.

When I was first brought to this bed the tree-tops were flowing with summer green. I had watched those heart-shaped leaves fulfil their golden destiny. I had watched them shiver away, one by one, until there were only three leaves left. Three leaves, two leaves, and by Christmas one leaf beat against the bough. It made me think of a despairing, imprisoned bird. That was a year ago. In the spring all the young leaves had come trooping back and burst into life. Once more I saw them flame and die until there were but four leaves left. Four leaves, three leaves, and now on Christmas morning two leaves scraped together on their lonely bough. I had counted time not by days but by seasons, and the poplars had been my dial.

But there were other leaves to tell the time this morning. All over the ward twined glossy holly. Its red berries fairly tinkled from the door through which might come at any moment she for whom I waited.

A swish of white—but it was only Miss Sally May, the brown-eyed nurse from Baltimore, with a pitcher of water. Lifting the bowl from my stand to a little chair which she pushed beside the bed, she filled it with water.

"Suh proud and hotty since he washes his own face that he hardly notices his old friends," Miss Sally confided to the pitcher as she handed me my wash-cloth and towel.

"I know a certain young southern belle that had better keep from under the mistletoe to-day," I in my turn confided to the bowl while my face glowed with cold water.

My eyes, answering the challenge in hers, caught another gleam of white at the door. It was hard to bring the proper earnestness to a flirtation, even with a Baltimore girl, when my heart waited for the opening of the swinging door. But it was only a nurse from another ward; and after brushing my teeth and letting Miss Sally May take my pulse, I settled back on the pillow that she had freshened for me. René, the most lively of the convalescents, pushed a basket of cigarettes under my nose. Lighting one, I lay back and amused myself by sending out smoke-rings from both corners of my mouth. And between the two curling streamers of smoke that floated away like incense from a Buddha's lips, my half-closed eyes watched for a white skirt, whiter than any other skirt.

On this Christmas morning as I waited for her to enter the swinging-door, there was none of the old anguish in my desire. And as she came at last down the ward, stopping here and there on the way to me, only a spirit of content was in my watching. It was too utterly sweet that she should be here in this room, that I could look at her as she bent over that one grizzled French captain, that I could catch the eager, grateful smile with which another officer looked up at her.

When she did at last reach my side, she looked down at me with a swift little smile.

"Good morning, Merry Christmas, will you dine with me to-night?"

My own words to her of that other Christmas two years before! Two things beat against my heart at the words. One, a wayward triumph that she should have remembered so exactly; the other, a pain that she should thus remind me of the change.

She seemed to see only the latter and a hot little flush mounted her cheek to the first wave of crisp black hair showing under the nurse's cap. "Oh, no, no, no," she whispered, "how could you think—that? I'm not making fun. I'm really asking you. Listen, my dear, the doctor has said so—you are to try walking this day. That is your Christmas present."

I stared at her incredulously. It had been almost sixteen months since the great surgeon, grey and grave and steady, had promised to try getting me out of this bed. Now for the first time I had been delivered from the long course of scientific treatments he had prescribed. Only yesterday the tight plaster cast had been removed and I had not yet dared to hope for that day when I should at last get up from this prison bed. God, could it be true! I lay there tossed between fear and hope. What if I couldn't—after all, what if I couldn't? I began to almost dread the test ahead of me. During all these months I had tried to school myself to the worst, to a future where I should be walked and never walk. Now, however—I felt that defeated hope would kill me.

"Oh, yes, and here's another Christmas gift," I heard my nurse's voice saying and she put into my hand a heavy square white envelope.

The moment I saw the type of stationery and the big wayward hand in which my name was written, I knew what it was and from whom it came. Jasmine! Her wedding announcement! And I did not need to open the envelope to find out that Lee Malone's name was inside.

It was the first time I had heard from her since that Christmas two years ago when she had sent me her photograph. I had never acknowledged the gift simply because every time I tried to do so Eileen Gale's face came between me and the page and made every word sound as if a stranger were writing down words to another stranger. Nor had my mother ever mentioned Jasmine. Perhaps she had fancied that the only news she could give of her would wound me. So, like a genii from the sea, leaped out this ghost of an old intense life.

"Mr. and Mrs. Sefton Grey announce the marriage of their daughter Jasmine——" In a stupor I read the engraved announcement. Then in one gusty minute the stupor was pricked. A magnolia dipping in the breeze shuttered her face from the moonlight. In that kind darkness I groped for her soft lips with my own—groped and found them. My heart sang in triumph at that first kiss. She was mine. The earth was mine. The old passion whirled upon me—whirled and bore me down. It came from my memory of Jasmine Grey, but it took me to Eileen Gale.

"Why, what is it? What has happened?" I heard her whisper in alarm.

I forced a smile. "Oh," I answered at last, "I suppose it's never pleasant to hear that your old love has married the other fellow."

I saw something cross her face. The something went through me fierily. "Eileen," I whispered savagely, "God, don't you see?" And I closed my eyes against the racking vision of what could never be—of meeting Eileen Gale's lips with my own. I forgot all the contentment in her mere presence which I had learned. I wanted her, wanted her, wanted her. And so long had I thought of myself as incurably helpless that it was a moment before her first words came back to me. If I should really be able to walk again—ah, then, the vision might not be so impossible—I opened upon her eyes haggard with hope.

She had made no reply to my words. She was just standing there with her hands folded and her eyes fixed quietly—almost gravely—on my face. Had she understood what I was trying to tell her? Before I could decide she was gone.

Half an hour later she was bringing Christmas to our ward. There was a tree webbed in tinsel, glittering with American ornaments, and she wheeled it to the bedside of each patient. It was strange, but at the sight of that tree I forgot all deeper things. Christmas is always a separate place. It is the great meeting-ground of childhood and maturity. To the sick man its magic is even brighter. As the eye of all of us wounded men followed the tree we left behind us every other thought. And afterwards when Miss Gale took from the fir-boughs presents for each patient, the eyes of these soldiers grew big with suspense as those of children.

"But how did you know I wanted this? And

this? And this?" There were excited cries all over the room. I myself could just hardly wait until that tree came up to my bed.

But when it did come, she took down for me only one small package. With fingers that were trembling with excitement, I took off the red ribbons, I unwrapped fold after fold of white tissue paper. I came at last to my gift. It was merely a card on which were written the words, "Please call for package at the office of Miss Gale."

I frowned a little. It was so bright and cosy here in this house of Christmas that I hated to be reminded of graver issues. "Do I have to try to walk—to-day?" I pleaded.

"Hmph!" she addressed the Christmas tree, "he doesn't want to walk. He wants his Christmas to walk."

In a few moments she came back with a pair of crutches. The head surgeon was with her. So were Miss Sally May and another nurse. I began to tremble from head to foot.

They lifted me up in the bed. They put my feet on the floor. They raised me up. The room raced madly around my head—the cots with their outspread Christmas treasure of books and fruit and neckties were mere dizzy spots. Then as my head began to clear the furniture and the figures

about me which had loomed so large above my bed
for many months were all dwarfed to their actual
size.

"Now, take a step," urged the head surgeon.

I was terrified. Sweat broke out on my forehead. Even to stand with the support of four
people was unbelievable effort.

"I can't," I cried.

Meanwhile all my fellow-patients had been
staring at me with the gibing curiosity which we
all exercised upon convalescents.

"*Sacré!* Bounds like an antelope," cried out a
one-armed young lieutenant who had bound his
new red silk necktie about the bandage on his
forehead.

"Look out there, he'll run away from you,"
added another.

While the rest of them were contributing that
joking comment of which I have already spoken
as being so dear to the heart of the wounded soldier, I tried to take that step. I plunged forward. They all pulled me back. I tried again.
It was no use. Muscles unused for eighteen
months had forgotten how to obey my will.

"Give it up," I panted. " 'S no use."

They lifted me into a wheel-chair and as Miss
Gale pushed me out to her office I had to set my

teeth to keep from crying. When I finally arrived there, I leaned back in my chair and closed my eyes. I had been prostrated by those poor efforts at walking, I could not speak.

Through the terrible black weakness I heard her voice more tender than it had ever been. "Why, they all have to learn over again," it was saying.

I roused myself. "Don't," I cried fiercely, "I can't stand your pity."

For a moment she said nothing. "Pity!" she repeated at last and I heard her give a soft little laugh. "Pity, why, how—funny!"

Another instant and the crisp little figure moved across the room with the springy step that I knew so well. She pulled aside a screen and in stupefied silence I watched her roll out a table which, blazing with poinsettias and candles, looked exactly the same as that secluded corner table in the unsecluded café where I had taken her two years before. Without a word she pulled the table in front of me. Then, darkening the room so that the candles were now our only light, she sat down opposite to me and as we waited Antoinette brought in our soup.

Feeling as if I were in a dream I took a first taste of that soup.

"Why, it's potage Margerole," I cried, "the

very same we had that night! How did you remember that?"

Her face broke into the familiar nooks and crannies. In each one of them you found some different thing—wistfulness, gaiety, a mocking tenderness—in a haze I saw them all. And as I did so headlong triumph—a triumph I had thought would never be mine—made me forget all that I should have remembered.

"Oh, you must have—just a little—or else you wouldn't have remembered everything just as it was—the poinsettias—the candles—even the soup." I heard the words being said by some one.

For reply, she put her elbows on the snowy table-cloth and leaned across to me. "Dear, foolish Swallow," she whispered.

"Honestly?" I said breathlessly.

"Honestly," said she, "from the very first moment I saw you."

I looked into the bending Heaven of her face. "But why?" I asked. "Oh, it can't be true. Your swallow can't fly any more, you know."

"Ah, but that is what you can—always," said she, her face alight with something I had never seen. "There's something in you that will keep going on. First you took to wings of steel. That was a boy's adventure—the adventure of the

body. Then began the real adventure—of the
spirit. Oh, Swallow, don't you think I haven't
seen—all your flying—all these months in bed."

Her words exalted me. Then came the old
weighting sense of what I really was, of the mean-
ness of accepting such happiness.

"Eileen, Eileen," I groaned, "I can't take it—
not when I'm like this—just something to be sorry
for."

"Sorry!" she flung back my word stormily. "Of
course I'm sorry for all you've suffered. But do
you think I could pity you for the way you've
suffered? Why, do you imagine I would have let
you have that morphine if I had thought you were
weak?"

I looked at her in amazement. "What do you
mean?" I groped.

"I mean that I did not tell Dr. Olson that time
when I found you had had it smuggled to you just
because I trusted you to break off. You did break
it off, too. I saw you struggling—it just broke my
heart.—Pity? Could any one pity a man like
you?"

I had thought that I had learned to understand
her. Now I saw that all my life I was going to
be following her, humbly, along new, hidden
paths.

"Oh, Stormy Petrel," I cried, and in the cry was gathered up all the reverence I had ever felt, "I can't be sorry for myself when being sick has shown me you. Two years ago to-day I fell in love with you. In a queer callow way I sort of divined everything that made you different. Of course, you were pretty and charming, but that wasn't it. There were things you stood for—just the way you always understood—somehow you were never forcing your charm and good looks— like—like——" I stopped myself just in time to avoid Jasmine's name. Then reaching for her hand under the fire of poinsettias, I finished solemnly. "I guess maybe that's what the war has done for a lot of us. It's made us care for a different thing in women."

She gave my fingers a little tender pressure, but to her eyes came back the old mocking laugh. "Dear, dear," said she, "and to think that I first liked him because he didn't know anything about women."

It was after I had been taken back into the ward that the head surgeon gave me my great Christmas present. This was the assurance that, in spite of my dismal failure that morning, I would walk again, with only a heavy limp and a cane between me and normal activity.

As if this was not enough, this tremulous, blinding hope of a happiness I had forsworn, Eileen came to take me for an outing. Bundling me up in my old military coat from which the blood had been cleaned, she pinned my medals on my breast, stuck my "berry" on my head, rolled me out of the ward with its festive burden of holly and mistletoe, rolled me down into the court. For the first time in eighteen months I was in the open air! ' My excitement was so painful that to calm me she let the hospital boy wheel me while she walked by my side.

"Look! Look!" I cried, as we made our way to the street. "A dog!"

She laughed. I had forgotten there were dogs. I had forgotten there were children or street-cars or automobiles or anything but beds and operating-tables, doctors and dressings. How wonderful to begin life again in the winy December sunshine! Not the storm-spent joy of a sail in wind and rain, not a billowy gallop across the prairies, not even that first triumphant flight above the clouds—nothing had ever been so intoxicating as this ride through the Bois in an old wheel-chair.

Evening mist began to rise. The sun was setting red and moist through the fog like a large, ripe fruit. Velvet evergreens dripped with moss.

Oaks spread out their bare, dark boughs. They looked as if their roots were in the air.

"I wonder if they're standing on their heads, those oaks," I mused.

She laughed again. I looked up at her as she stepped along beside me, at her cheeks as red as the sun going down through the mist, at eyes always laughing away something deeper than laughter, at the dancing waves of hair, young despite those little spots of grey that had come with her decoration for brave service.

I knew that I should sleep that night deliciously. I knew that I should be walking soon. I hoped—and it has happened since—that my mother would see me not creeping on crutches but in the service of my country. Youth and strength came singing back to me. "Home, now, Pierre," she said.

"Home, now, Pierre," I repeated, still looking at her.

CPSIA information can be obtained at www.ICGtesting.com
Printed in the USA
LVOW01s0748020514

384176LV00003B/421/P